PACKER & SONS

By Tommy Murphy

BELVOIR

CURRENCY PRESS
The performing arts publisher

CURRENT THEATRE SERIES

First published in 2019
by Currency Press Pty Ltd,
Gadigal Land, Suite 310, 46-56 Kippax Street, Surry Hills NSW 2010 Australia
enquiries@currency.com.au
www.currency.com.au

in association with Belvoir, Sydney

First revised edition published in 2019.

Typeset by Dean Nottle for Currency Press.
Cover image shows Kerry Packer, photograph by Peter Morris/Fairfax Syndication.
Cover design by Alphabet Studios.
A catalogue record of this title is available from the National Library of Australia: www.nla.gov.au
Currency Press acknowledges the Traditional Owners of the Country on which we live and work. We pay our respects to all Aboriginal and Torres Strait Islander Elders, past and present.

Contents

For Philip, my loving father.

Playwright's note

James Packer believes you want to be him. 'I recognise that the vast majority of people would swap places with me and I wouldn't swap places with—with anyone'.[1] Is he right?

Trade places. Imagine what you would do with your billions, your birthright. Admit the luxuries you'd indulge. Envisage the social good you would achieve. Now, what obligation would you feel to extend the family project? It is a fortune built on the stewardship, chiefly, of media assets for over a century. You are its fourth monarch. Every preceding Packer has managed an expansion adapted for a new era. Do it your way. Seek trusty advisors; the best money can provide. Whose influence might you buy? In your mansion, on your icebreaker-cum-ocean-leisure-cruiser furnished with cinema and helipad, consider whether you have enough.

There is one further condition. You have Kerry Packer as your father.

Goya, the great Spanish painter, depicted the eternal risk of fatherhood. He has the old man holding a child to his face, not to kiss it or admire it but to devour. The head's but an appetiser; he's gnawing an arm. It's an act of compulsive infanticide—yet his eyes convey shame. This is not Kerry; this is the Roman god, Saturn, tormented by a prophecy that he would be overthrown by his offspring. Drastic action. Goya has the father naked, his groin pronounced. He reminds us that the competition between father and offspring is a crisis of masculinity.

Right now a casino tower grows on our city's skyline. As the casino plans were unveiled, James told Mike Willesee, 'I think that in a funny way doing something in Sydney really—this might sound like a funny thing to say—but I think it ticks the final box in me being my own man. Being my own man. There's a big shadow. There's a big shadow.' The picture of Sydney will be forever altered to reflect that desire.

Anyway you look at it, young Packer got special treatment to erect his latest skyscraper. The approvals process was accelerated. The rule

---

1 'Sunday Night', Channel 7 interview with Michael Willesee, 2013.

that Sydney would only ever have one casino was rescinded. Land set aside at Barangaroo for public use was reconfigured. James proclaimed, 'If I don't finish Sydney, that will be the end of me.'[2]

Earlier this year, James became the highest-ranking Australian business person to go public about personal mental health battles. He was rightfully applauded for that brave act. He withdrew from the board of Crown Resorts to receive treatment. As this play reaches the stage in November 2019, James is seeking to sell his stake in the business that he reshaped from his family fortune—no longer media but gambling. His withdrawal leaves serious questions about the future corporate responsibility of Crown and its Sydney Casino development. Allegations were recently raised that Crown Resorts profited from improper activity by consular officials and allowed passage of organised crime and money laundering. James Packer has denied any knowledge of that criminality.

This play is not the casino narrative. That story is yet unwritten. And then, perhaps it's already etched into history. Like all things Packer, the echoes with the past resound.

> I have heard him charged with being too tough, or too rough in his treatment of people. My answer has always been, and still is, that all his faults are masculine.
> *Former Prime Minister Robert Menzies of Sir Frank Packer*

> There's only one way I know how to manage people: through fear.
> *Kerry Packer*

Packer & Sons is an origin story of the man beneath the casino tower, told via three generations and their cycles of patriarchal brutality. It intends to examine male privilege in our society and an entitlement to take from others.

Despite all, do you still want to be him?

---

2   Damon Kitney, *The Price of Fortune*, Harper Collins, 2018.

Thank you

Packer & Sons reaches the stage via the David Williamson Prize for Excellence in Writing for Australian Theatre, which was awarded to Belvoir in 2018 in acknowledgment of Leah Purcell's excellent play *The Drover's Wife*. The prize money was granted to the company on the condition that they usher a new play into being. This is that play and I am honoured to have been trusted to write it. The award was made possible by a generous donation from David and Kristin Williamson and Shane and Cathryn Brennan and is administered by The Australian Writers' Guild, of which I am a proud member.

I am indebted to Eamon Flack, Louise Gough, Sue Donnelly, the cast, stage management and entire Belvoir team and the board led by Sam Meers.

I, along with Belvoir, gratefully acknowledge that aspects of this play are inspired by Paul Barry's books, *The Rise and Rise of Kerry Packer* and *Rich Kids*. I thank Paul for his time and response to the play.

My gratitude also goes to Bridget Griffen-Foley, author and academic, for guiding me on my research and for her excellent writings on the Packers. Helen Grasswill and Greg Hassall at *Australian Story* kindly shared with me their wealth of research.

I am grateful for the assistance of Anita Jacoby, Francis Packer, Christoph Klimmer, Mark Riley, Sally Virgoe, Aaron Patrick, Damon Kitney, the staff at the State Library of NSW, Gus Murray, Peter Meakin, Adele Ferguson, Terence Clarke, Hammer Dixon, Paddy Murphy, David Berthold, Alex McClintock, Michael Shea, Allyn and Alana Hicks, Nick 'Noodle' Swift, Rohit Biswas, Angela Bowne, Catherine Dovey, Kim Williams, Richard Cottrell, John Turnbull and those I interviewed who requested not to be named.

Packer & Sons was completed during a residency at Currency Press. Thanks to Claire Grady, Deborah Franco, Lucy Wirth, Nick Parsons, Katharine Brisbane and the Currency team. Thank you to my fellow writers Suzie Miller, Katie Pollock and Alison Lyssa for their advice, Baker & McKenzie lawyers and to my agent Anthony Blair at Cameron Creswell.

I also thank my ever-loving family, especially my late father, Philip, for his contrasting story of paternal love and to whom this play is dedicated. And to the late Dane Crawford, my life partner: *Thank you for the meal you cooked the night we thought this project had fallen over and for the nourishment you will always give, darl.*

Tommy Murphy, November 2019

Packer & Sons was first performed by Belvoir at Belvoir St Theatre, Sydney, on 20 November, 2019, with the following cast:

YOUNG RUPERT MURDOCH / LACHLAN MURDOCH / OTHERS	Nick Bartlett
RUPERT MURDOCH / NICK FALLOON / OTHERS	John Gaden
JODEE RICH / OTHERS	Anthony Harkin
OLDER KERRY PACKER / FRANK PACKER	John Howard
CLYDE PACKER / OTHERS	Brandon McClelland
JAMES PACKER / YOUNGER KERRY PACKER	Josh McConville
BOY JAMES / BOY KERRY	Nate Sammut
BOY JAMES / BOY KERRY	Byron Wolffe

Director, Eamon Flack
Set and Costume Designer, Romanie Harper
Lighting Designer, Nick Schlieper
Composer, Alan John
Sound Designer, David Bergman and Steve Francis
Movement and Fight Director, Nigel Poulton
Assistant Director, Hannah Goodwin
Interim Production Manager, Ren Kenward
Props Supervisor, Jessica Martin
Costume Co-ordinator, Jacqueline Lucey
Chaperone, Jai Greenaway
Stage Manager, Luke McGettigan
Assistant Stage Manager, Jen Parsonage

Supported by the Australian Writers' Guild's David Williamson Prize, The Copyright Agency Cultural Fund, and the Walking Up the Hill Foundation.

ROLES

1. JAMES PACKER, YOUNG KERRY PACKER.
2. OLDER KERRY PACKER, FRANK PACKER.
3. PARAMEDIC, CLYDE PACKER, NURSE, EXECUTIVE NAMED DANIEL, LACHLAN'S BUTLER/GHOST, ENSEMBLE.
4. PARAMEDIC, RUPERT MURDOCH, NICK FALLOON, DOCTOR BOB WRIGHT, PBL LAWYER, ENSEMBLE.
5. POLO PLAYER, THUG, YOUNG RUPERT MURDOCH, LACHLAN MURDOCH, ENSEMBLE.
6. EMPLOYEE ON POLO FIELD, THUG, BARRY KNIGHT, JODEE RICH, ENSEMBLE.
7. BOY JAMES, BOY KERRY.

This play went to press before the end of rehearsals and may differ from the play as performed.

ACT ONE

SCENE ONE

A field. A large man astride a horse.

The man slumps forward, dead. The horse awaits commands from the rider, halted in the middle of the field.

The man is KERRY PACKER. *He has had a heart attack. He is in polo gear.*

JAMIE PACKER *(later known as* JAMES*), aged 23, races to the scene. He is also in polo gear.*

JAMIE: Dad. Fuck. Christ. Dad.

> *He pulls at his father's bulk but cannot manage the dismount alone. Other* MEN *from the Ellerston White Polo Team arrive.*

Ambulance. Please. Quick.

PLAYER 1: Called, Jamie. It's called.

JAMIE: The one that was here? And Dad's chopper?

PLAYER 2: I think someone—

JAMIE: Check. Please. Signal for the chopper.

> *He directs the* MEN *as they take* KERRY *down from his horse.*

Easy, go easy.

PLAYER 1: We're right, Jamie. We've got him.

> JAMIE *makes a chopper motion, then bangs his own chest, to signal to people far away, as the* PLAYERS *commence cardiac massage on* KERRY.

JAMIE: [*to others approaching*] Chopper. Get the chopper. Please.

PLAYER 1: He's not good, Jamie.

JAMIE: He's going to be fine. I want Victor Chang.

> *Another man, an* EMPLOYEE, *runs a large early-model mobile phone to* JAMIE. *This is 1990.*

Does it have a signal? These portable phones are useless. Go to the pavilion. Get to a proper phone. Or try a car phone. Get into my car for a phone. Please. Get Nick Ross in the chopper. Radio for Chang. Ross can radio Saint Vincent's. It's going to be his heart. This is his heart. Tell that chick there to stay off the field in her high heels. Tell her to piss off back to the pavilion; we've got enough people here.

He hands back the phone.

I need a phone that works please. Anyone sees arseholes with cameras you find out who they work for, you get their names and their editor's name and you keep them pinned. Your jobs depend on that. You, you get me David Leckie at Channel Nine. And you get me Dad's physician—Bob Wright's his name. [*To the* MEN *reviving his father*] You doing that right: four breaths, is it four breaths to every pump? Who can verify these guys are doing CPR right? You, get down and help please. There was an ambulance on the other side of the track. Who saw where it went?

EMPLOYEE: We've called an ambulance, Jamie.

JAMIE: We need that ambulance that was here. Someone control the fuckin' horses over there. Please.

PLAYER 1: I didn't see an ambulance here.

JAMIE: Didn't we have one on call for the match?

PLAYER 2: No.

JAMIE: Why not? Who plans that? How's he looking?

PLAYER 2: Don't worry, mate. We've called one.

JAMIE: Okay thank you but I just want you to get over there and ask where that ambulance went. [*Seeing his father's state*] Dad, come on, I love you, hold on. Please not yet. We're getting an ambulance. Get me that ambulance!

PLAYER 2: There's nothing you can do to make it come sooner.

JAMIE: There. Look. What's that there? A block of flats? That's the fucking ambulance I saw. Are you blokes fuckin' listening to me?

Two PARAMEDICS *run to* KERRY.

Are you the ambos we've called?

PARAMEDIC 1: No but we were passing the gates. You're very lucky, mate.

The PARAMEDICS *work to assess and revive* KERRY.

JAMIE: My father is fifty-two years old—fifty-three in December—he has had three heart attacks prior. What other medical history do you need? He hasn't been drinking. Doesn't drink at all. He is a smoker. He's not responding and we've checked his airways and—these blokes know CPR. They've been—

PARAMEDIC 2: Thanks. We'll take care of it, mate.

JAMIE: Thanks. He hasn't complained today of any—

PARAMEDIC 2: Mate, just stand back now. We've got it under control.

JAMIE: Sure. I'm getting his cardiologist, Victor Chang, to come straight away.

PARAMEDIC 1: He's here, is he?

JAMIE: He'll meet us at Saint Vincent's. He'll fly in—he's in Japan or somewhere. We knew that.

PARAMEDIC 2: Yeah, we're taking him to the district hospital.

JAMIE: No you're not. I'm getting him choppered to Saint Vincent's. It's being arranged now. Bob Wright's been notified at Vincent's. [*To the others*] That's right? Bob knows?

> PARAMEDIC 1 *pounds* KERRY*'s chest with increasing urgency.* PARAMEDIC 2 *holds an oxygen mask to his face.*

We're getting the chopper in.

PARAMEDIC 2: Careflight? They're not going to come for this, mate. He'll be dead if we don't take him. It's alright.

JAMIE: How is it? He can't die.

PARAMEDIC 2: You can sit in the back of the ambulance with your dad if you like.

JAMIE: Mate? Don't you know who this is?

> *The helicopter approaches.*

This man is Kerry Packer.

> *A helicopter hammers loudly above them as the device they've strapped to his chest jolts his body. The chopper lashes the wind into a vortex ... transporting us to another time.*
>
> *A young boy in cricket gear stands in an open field. Lost, alone, ` waiting. And then ...*

SCENE TWO

Two THUGS *bash a young man. Their victim is* YOUNG KERRY PACKER. *He is played by the same actor who played* JAMES *in the first scene. Doubling of this nature continues throughout the play.*

THUG # 1: [*hitting* KERRY] Enough. Enough. Enough. No more excuses. Don't wanna hear no more—

> KERRY *hurls vomit.*

Christ.

THUG # 2: We do that?

THUG # 1: Nah, he's just—he's drunk—you alright, Kerry?

KERRY: No I'm bloody not.

> KERRY *coughs and splutters, trying to spew.*

THUG # 2: He's faking.

THUG # 1: We're going to keep on hitting you, Kerry.

KERRY: You want my father to see what you've done to me?

THUG # 2: If he's gonna pay your gambling debts.

KERRY: You'd be dealing with harder boys. My old man has harder boys he will call.

> THUG # 1 *slaps* KERRY. *Open palm, slap and slap.* KERRY *buckles and shields himself.*

THUG # 1: Cheeky rich bastard.

> THUG # 2 *joins the slapping. A voice calls to them.*

CLYDE: Leave him. That's enough.

> CLYDE PACKER *has appeared. He wears a crisp shirt and black tie. It is the mid 1950s.*

THUG # 1: Who are you?

CLYDE: He owe you money?

THUG # 1: Who are you first?

CLYDE: Kerry, do you owe these men money?

KERRY: They wanna kill me.

THUG # 2: Do not. Want you to pay.

CLYDE: How much?

THUG # 1: Enough to buy a house, a nice one.

THUG # 2: Plus interest.

KERRY: Interest?

CLYDE: SP bookies sent you. Is that what this is?

THUG # 2: Yeah. Real cranky ones. He owes them fifteen thousand.

CLYDE: Holy hell.

KERRY: Rot.

A swift punch to KERRY.

THUG # 1: You're his mate?

CLYDE: I'm his brother.

THUG # 1: You wan' a floggin' too?

CLYDE: No. I do not. That amount of money, that's a big sum, I will need to speak to my bank manager.

THUG # 1: My arse.

He kicks KERRY.

CLYDE: Hey, hey. Give me tomorrow to do that. You come to me in Bellevue Hill.

KERRY: Don't tell 'em where we live.

CLYDE: They'll soon work it out.

THUG # 2: Yeah, nah, we know. Big place. About ten houses.

CLYDE: Three homes. Cairnton, on Victoria Road. There's a guardhouse at the gate. I'll have a chap stationed there. You'll get your money tomorrow evening.

THUG # 1: Or we'll be coming for you too.

CLYDE: You can trust me. I do have one condition: you and your associates are never to accept a bet from Kerry Francis Bullmore Packer again in your careers.

KERRY, *drunk and wounded, makes an attempt to strike* THUG # 1 *in the back of the head but is collected by* THUG # 2.

THUG # 2: You don't get to punch us, Kerry. You have our employer's money. You don't get to do what you like.

THUG # 1 *lays into* KERRY *for good measure.*

CLYDE: Leave him. You've made your point.

KERRY: That all you got?

CLYDE: Shoosh, Kerry.

KERRY: That all you—?

THUG # 2 *hits* KERRY.

THUG # 2: No, it's not all we've got. You want more? Hey?

KERRY: Nah. Nah, no more.

KERRY *laughs.*

CLYDE: You'll get your money. You have my word.

THUG # 2: We'll be there tomorrow night, chubs.

> *The two* THUGS *leave as* KERRY *tugs a hip flask from his clothing and swigs.*

CLYDE: This ends, Kerry.

KERRY: They got me pretty good.

CLYDE: Who's going to bail you out when I'm in Cambridge?

KERRY: I had a losing streak.

CLYDE: No, it ends. Jesus, Kero. There is only so much I can do to stop him finding out.

KERRY: Yeah, well, don't let that happen.

CLYDE: I ought to.

KERRY: You wouldn't.

CLYDE: I jolly well will tell Dad if you don't pay me back.

KERRY: Yeah I—

CLYDE: No no, you will this time, Kerry. I'll have Philip draw up a loan between us because I can't afford this, not on the pittance Dad pays us. And, and what if a Fairfax photographer had seen this? Hey?

KERRY: Nobody knows who I am.

CLYDE: Don't you be so sure. They know who I am. They do actually. And they know you're a complete embarrassment.

KERRY: Ha. You think you're him?

CLYDE: No. Dad would have let them wallop you a lot longer.

KERRY: [*with a laugh*] Yeah. He woulda. They did get me pretty good.

CLYDE: You need a doctor?

KERRY: No no, I'm—

CLYDE: Well now, I am wondering if that one there needs a stitch maybe.

KERRY: I know how to roll with a punch. Wanna go find where they went?

CLYDE: No.

> KERRY *swigs his drink.*

Stop that. You're inebriated enough.

KERRY: 'Inebriated'. Phhh. Wait a minute while I—

> KERRY *pisses.*

CLYDE: Don't do that here.

KERRY: What's your elitist word for piddle, Clyde?

CLYDE: I don't know.

KERRY: Piss-a-piss-a, what's the word?

CLYDE: Micturate.

KERRY: Is it?

CLYDE: Think so.

> KERRY *laughs at* CLYDE.

Car's waiting around the corner. Are you able to walk?

KERRY: I'm not going home yet.

CLYDE: Yes. You are.

KERRY: Charged up. Going whoring.

CLYDE: You're broke.

KERRY: Madam keeps an account for me.

> *He wipes his hands on himself.* KERRY *clambers off.*

CLYDE: Kerry? Kerry. Kerry, are you honestly walking off on me?

KERRY: Come with me if you like.

CLYDE: I don't rescue you so you can just … It doesn't work like that. Kerry? Kerry.

> KERRY *meanders drunk, tripping up and falling, yet pushing on. Drunk, very drunk, alone on the streets.*

SCENE THREE

YOUNG KERRY PACKER *is in hospital with a dressing on his forehead. A voice bellows for him.*

FRANK: [*offstage*] Kerry! Kerry! Where is he?

> KERRY *winces. Dad's coming for him.*

Kerry! Where is he in this damn—damn maze?! Kerry, you answer me, son.

> CLYDE *enters in a coat. He looks to* KERRY, *inhales. Their father approaches.*

Kerry! Where? Where?

CLYDE: Dad. In here. He's in here. I found him.

> FRANK PACKER *enters in hat, coat and spectacles.*

FRANK: You've done it now, son. Really done it now.

KERRY: Dad—

FRANK: I'm speaking.

KERRY: Yes, Dad.

FRANK: Stand up.

KERRY: I can't.

FRANK: Stand up and greet your father.

CLYDE: Dad, he's hurt. He's…

FRANK: What did you say, Fatty?

CLYDE: No, I …

KERRY: I have a broken hip.

FRANK: Now? You've done this to me now, on the eve of everything I am achieving? I was dragged from an appointment with Menzies to be with you, son. I warn you, this new venture could sink. It is twelve weeks' wages for an ordinary man to go out and buy the appliance. If television fails to catch on, you boys will have nothing and I'll be dead with a heart attack. I've already outlived my father.

CLYDE: Dad, do you want a cigarette?

FRANK: Want? A cigarette? No I do not.

KERRY: I would.

FRANK: Don't you test me, boy. I decide when we make a prime minister wait. Not you and your—inabilities.

KERRY: I know I make you angry but—

FRANK: Oh, you know, do you? Goading me then, are you? Leaving light globes burning in the blinking house and now a smashed-up sports car.

KERRY: It's not the sports car. It was Mrs Ash's car. It's a write-off.

FRANK: Oh, you're paying for it, my boy.

KERRY: But I—

FRANK: I've a good mind to leave my money to the church, not pour it out on Dumb-Dumb's wreckages and your—your international travel, Fatty.

CLYDE: I've done nothing wrong.

FRANK: I beg your pardon.

CLYDE: I am standing by you.

FRANK: You'd better, I say, because your younger brother is a dolt.

KERRY: I'm lucky to be alive.

FRANK: I doubt that, Kerry. You can't just go to the *Telegraph*'s police roundsmen this time—or whomever it is that's been vanishing your speeding fines. You've been caught. And I know you sleep on the job.

KERRY: No—

CLYDE: You do, Kerry. You kip in the paper bales.

KERRY: Why'd you tell him that?

FRANK: This is the end, Kerry. It's done. I'm done. I have a job for you as a jackeroo.

KERRY: I almost died. Honestly. I could have died. The constable said to me this was the worst motor vehicle accident he's ever seen.

FRANK: Were you at fault?

KERRY: I nearly died.

FRANK: But was it your fault?

KERRY: It was a stretch of, really, a practically straight bit of road. And these headlights—they were drifting towards me and, and coming right at me. I was on the left. I was. I dipped my lights and I moved over and he kept coming at me—I was cruising at fifty—and at the last moment I tried to swerve … The Rover Ninety is a good vehicle but the other car … it didn't come off so well … an Austin I think … I went … I …

FRANK: Yes? String a sentence along.

KERRY: The cigarette please. My nerves are shot.

They ignore his request.

It was raining and I went over—somehow because my leg was … And I saw … the driver was younger than me. Three in the car. Three school-aged boys. One seemed small. His ear had all this blood and the way his eyes had gone … Dead, Dad. They are all dead. Three young men. Dead.

Silence.

FRANK: How would you know if it was fifty miles you were cruising at? Don't mention that. It sounds like a lie.

KERRY: It isn't.

FRANK: It's how it'll be perceived. You better tell us how much you told the police.

KERRY: They asked if I might have dozed off.

FRANK: You hadn't.

KERRY: I had slept before I took over driving. Mrs Ash had told me to walk around a little in the cold night air. It woke me up so I was good to drive.

FRANK: Has Mrs Ash spoken to the police?

KERRY: Yes, but she was asleep when we crashed and doesn't recall. Mrs Ash was pinned in her seat. She's in a bad way.

FRANK: No other witnesses.

KERRY: None … living.

FRANK: Clyde, I'll need to get word to the other proprietors. Track down Warwick Fairfax. And the local rags: the *Goulburn Post*, *Monaro Post*. Find a telephone here. Mention the personal toll, Kerry's innocence. A private matter. I'll have to have a think about which silk. The premier ought to know who to brief.

CLYDE: And the police? He would have been drinking.

FRANK: No, no. That's not a problem.

KERRY: We had stopped at the Kosciusko Hotel and for dinner in Cooma.

FRANK: [*to* KERRY] Don't just go offering information, cretin. You weren't drinking, Kerry. Don't you know anything, Clyde?

CLYDE: Apparently not.

FRANK: Don't you play the clever dick with me, son.

CLYDE: Yes. Father.

KERRY: Dad, please, will you get me through this?

FRANK: Son, I doubt even I can do that. I pray there is some way out. You have excluded yourself from an important milestone. Packer is bringing television to Australia. All I can say on the matter is … there are people who create things, perhaps fifty or a hundred in every generation. You are not one of those people, Kerry. Your older brother at least has some nous. Clyde is staying in Australia to learn by my side.

CLYDE: Dad? I've already delayed my trip to help with the launch.

FRANK: There is no trip, Clyde.

CLYDE: I've been accepted into Cambridge.

FRANK: No, university will only make you a communist. Ten bob. It all started with ten bob on a Hobart racetrack and my father's lucky break. Don't you boys forget it. Good fortune could vanish just as quick.

KERRY: I'm sorry I've done this to you.

FRANK: No, you don't mean that.

> FRANK *abandons* KERRY.

CLYDE: Drag your arse on the bitumen, but don't you dare sick the bear onto me. I earned that place at Cambridge. You know what that is, Kerry? Earning a thing? No, but you'll cost me, happily enough.

KERRY: No. Not happily. [*Then* ...] Is mother coming to see me?

> *But he is alone.* CLYDE*'s cigarette is hanging from the edge of the ashtray with a trail of smoke, well out of reach.*
>
> KERRY *turns. The pain is severe. He angles towards the ashtray. He stands. A shot of pain. He hobbles. He gets himself that cigarette.*
>
> *The little boy waits on the cricket field.*

SCENE FOUR

> YOUNG KERRY PACKER *draws on a cigarette as he dresses into a dinner suit. His brother and father are nearby, also dressing.*

FRANK: [*to* CLYDE] What sort of capital raising?

CLYDE: Well, that—or make a change to operations.

FRANK: Tell. I am open to your ideas.

CLYDE: The *Telegraph* building alone, I bet if you leased it out you'd earn more.

FRANK: That's utter nonsense.

CLYDE: Right.

FRANK: Where would I produce my newspaper?

CLYDE: Alright. I actually think you should sell the *Telegraph*. We have television. We have—

FRANK: Clyde? I built it.

CLYDE: Sell a portion of it at least. With investment, a merger with another publisher, we could really stick it to Fairfax's *Granny Herald*.

FRANK: [*to* KERRY] Dumb-Dumb, pour a drink for us all before we get going.

CLYDE: I'd know just the partner to come on board, given the opportunity.

FRANK: Who?

CLYDE: Sir Keith Murdoch's son Rupert.

FRANK: No. You're not up to that.

CLYDE: We were banking on this new revenue coming in from the *Cosmopolitan* deal.

FRANK: We have other magazines. We have a far superior title.

CLYDE: For an older readership.

FRANK: I don't like this tone, boy. [*To* KERRY, *at the drinks trolley*] Don't drown it, Dumb-Dumb. Now, about tonight, something to sort out. I spoke to Menzies and—Where are my damn cufflinks?

> *They are in front of him.*

CLYDE: There.

FRANK: Where?

CLYDE: Just in front of you there.

> FRANK's *eyes are going.*

FRANK: Of course. Menzies says he'd prefer not to speak this evening. Retirement gave the poor devil this blasted paralysis of his face. I have asked that my sons present the medal to their father tonight instead. [*To* KERRY] Now, Dumb-Dumb, I see you baulk. You won't have to read. Just stand by Clyde and look intelligent. [*The drinks*] Not pouring yourself one?

KERRY: No, you know I've gone off it.

FRANK: Been a while.

KERRY: Yes.

FRANK: Well. See how you go tonight, hey.

KERRY: Yes, Dad.

FRANK: And if any smart Alec gets lippy about Fairfax nabbing this *Cosmopolitan* deal, you fellas set them straight. I never wanted it to succeed.

CLYDE: What, that's the official line, is it?

FRANK: It's the damn truth. I was only ever forcing Fairfax to overspend. I never wanted this crass American title in our stable.

CLYDE: You might have told me.

FRANK: What was that?

CLYDE: I led those negotiations. I was in it to win. How does that look for me now?

FRANK: And you didn't win. You didn't.

CLYDE: It cost us a very valuable reader: a young woman who isn't

after knitting patterns and the recipes of the *Women's Weekly*. The
royal family doesn't interest her either.

FRANK: I don't want the likes of her.

CLYDE: We want her money.

FRANK: What is this—this angst in you, Clyde? A grown man.

CLYDE: Am I?

KERRY: Just beat them to the newsstand. Churn out a copycat rag.

CLYDE: Right. Thanks for that, Kerry.

KERRY: Fairfax don't own all these eager young women. Give them a bit.

FRANK: A bit of what?

KERRY: A bit of biff.

CLYDE: What's the cricket score, Kero?

KERRY: What? I don't know.

CLYDE: You were sitting in front of the idiot box all day watching it.

KERRY: I was not.

FRANK: [*to* CLYDE] Is that what you think I am leading over there in
Willoughby, son? Idiot boxes?

CLYDE: Just a turn of phrase. I meant no offence.

FRANK: And as for you, Dumb-Dumb, you'll be back with the jackeroos
if I catch you watching the ABC in my building.

KERRY: It's rain delayed; I'm not even lying this time.

FRANK: Tell me, what's your reckoning on the cost of this 'bit of biff'?

KERRY: Well no, I just …

FRANK: Go on. It's your idea. You ought to back yourself up. What sort of
investment and resources would it take to launch a rival publication?

KERRY: Well … I'd have to look into it.

CLYDE: Yeah. You would.

KERRY: I just know it'd cost John Fairfax and Sons.

CLYDE: We ought to get going.

FRANK: Wait a minute. What would it cost them, Kerry?

KERRY: A clear shot at a new market—for which they overpaid.

> FRANK *chortles approvingly.*

CLYDE: I'll be happy to speak tonight. I'll pull together a few thoughts
in the car.

FRANK: I've written it for you. You just read it out for me. Why don't we
add to it that we'll change the name of the *Weekly* to the *Monthly*? A
sign we're able to modernise. Distract them from this other deal.

CLYDE: The '*Australian Women's Monthly*'?

FRANK: That's what it is now. Twelve yearly. Why not?

CLYDE: I think that's a—it has editorial implications.

FRANK: She's my brainchild. I'm not afraid to reposition her, to show my understanding of this modern woman. What do you think, Kerry?

KERRY: Me?

FRANK: Yes. I am asking your opinion, Dumb-Dumb.

KERRY: I reckon … Have Clyde announce it tonight. See how it lands.

SCENE FIVE

An anteroom at Sydney's Hordern Pavilion. It is 1972. YOUNG RUPERT MURDOCH *hands* YOUNG KERRY PACKER *a paper bag.*

RUPERT: There you are, Kerry.

KERRY: Appreciate it, Rupert.

RUPERT: Steak and kidney. That's what you wanted?

> *The bag contains a meat pie.*

KERRY: Nice, yeah.

RUPERT: Not having a lager or—?

KERRY: No, thank you. Just this.

RUPERT: You've had a success, Kerry: this new magazine.

KERRY: Always good to stick it to Fairfax, hey, Rupert. Take them by surprise.

RUPERT: You certainly did that. You stopped Sydney with that centrefold.

KERRY: Imagine my battle; my father refuses his journalists to even print the word 'lavatory'. I happen to understand this 1970s woman.

RUPERT: Do you let your wife read *Cleo*?

KERRY: Ros prefers the *Women's Weekly*.

RUPERT: Back in London Anna refuses to even touch the *Sun*.

KERRY: I'd like to touch your page three.

RUPERT: How's the pie?

KERRY: Bit frozen.

RUPERT: Don't eat it.

KERRY: Only the middle; edges alright. Excellent seats tonight, Rupert. Ringside. I got them through our sports editor at the *Sunday Telegraph*. Right in the guts of it.

RUPERT: My sports editor believes young Mundine is something of a sensation.

KERRY: A soft chin in my opinion. Denny Moyer fought Sugar Ray Robinson.

RUPERT: Ten years ago.

KERRY: How many rounds, Rupert? How much punishment can he take? Some can take a whack and some can't.

RUPERT: Fancy a wager?

KERRY: Twenty?

RUPERT: Make it fifty. One of us should walk away with something from tonight.

KERRY: Goodo. It was in fact my father who said I ought to take you to the match.

RUPERT: Yes?

KERRY: Dad has a plan—a proposal.

RUPERT: You need to raise funds at the *Telegraph*.

KERRY: No.

RUPERT: Yes you do.

KERRY: Dad wants me to gauge your interest in a partnership. You'd purchase forty-nine percent of the *Telegraphs*. Instead of Packer and Murdoch brawling, we'll put your *Daily Mirror* and the *Telegraphs* out of one office.

RUPERT: Your father was going to be forced to do something sooner or later.

KERRY: Not forced. An opportunity. *Cleo* magazine is just the beginning. We know we can stick it to Fairfax.

RUPERT: Tell him I don't see the sense in it: togetherness.

KERRY: Together we can compete against the *Herald*'s classifieds. With one building we'd reduce staff and costs. They'd be frightened. Dad has worked hard to keep you out. He'll let you in.

RUPERT: You don't know what I want.

KERRY: You want Sydney.

RUPERT: I have the *Mirror*. And blow Sydney. I am getting London.

KERRY: Have both.

RUPERT: How unwell is he, your father?

KERRY: Fit as a bull.

RUPERT: I know Sir Frank's eyes have gone. I have journalists who worked for him.

KERRY: Well they can't be trusted. Deserters.

RUPERT: You and Clyde have to protect yourself from bad advice. Make sure your stepmother is protected from it. That's a tip from the trenches when a father dies.

KERRY: Dad's not going anywhere.

RUPERT: Kerry, the *Telegraph* is run at a loss. Why would I want in?

KERRY: I thought you might have backed yourself to make something of it, Rupert.

> KERRY *licks his hands, has made a mess.*

RUPERT: Don't eat the frozen pie, Kerry. I'll sing out for the girl, get you another one.

KERRY: No no. Had enough. That does me.

> *He cleans himself up, licks his lips, his fingers.*

The *Telegraphs* bring my father something the *Women's Weekly* can never bring. Men. That is why you want in, Rupert. Influence.

RUPERT: It's an attractive title; you'll have other buyers.

KERRY: I think you'll regret this, Rupert.

RUPERT: Thanks for the tip. Reckon that's the bantamweight bashed. We should go down to the main match.

> RUPERT *starts to leave.*

KERRY: Take the *Telegraph*. Have it. A hundred percent.

> RUPERT *stops.*

Print it your way over at Surry Hills. Have the masthead. We keep the building.

RUPERT: Is that his offer?

KERRY: No. I'm asking that.

RUPERT: Well the old boy won't be too happy with you then.

KERRY: Unless you give me a price that'll stop him belting me.

RUPERT: He should name his price.

KERRY: He won't. He can't.

RUPERT: Why not?

KERRY: It'll break the old man's heart. Help me convince him.

RUPERT: Ha. That's all very well. Emotion.

KERRY: It's a real thing. The sale would see staff laid off. He's very loyal.

RUPERT: Kerry.

KERRY: He is loyal to his workers. You'd have to agree to take on a good portion of the staff.

RUPERT: You can't just foist staff on me.

KERRY: No, alright. Take your pick. But that's no small thing: giving you all that, that knowledge. And the remaining redundancies would be very costly for us so factor that in your price.

RUPERT: Look I think this is a very strange way to do business.

KERRY: We'd be making you formidable, Rupert. You'd have the *Daily Mirror* and the *Telegraphs* and we'd be out of the picture.

RUPERT: We best make our way down to the ring, Kerry.

KERRY: Unless I can take a price to my father, you forfeit this, Rupert. The *Telegraph* is a Sydney institution. My father acquired it at age thirty. He made it what it is. That's a lifetime's work. It's a brand that will outlive us all.

RUPERT: So why don't you want it?

KERRY: Because I think television is enough. Coupled with the magazines. So long as we provide what people actually want to see.

RUPERT: Your brother agree?

KERRY: Yes. He does in fact.

RUPERT: Is it fourteen?

> KERRY *laughs.*

Why are you laughing? That's a huge figure. It's got to be more than you expected.

KERRY: There's a history of heart trouble in the family. Is that what you're trying to do, make him keel over?

RUPERT: He might you know, Kerry. Think carefully about this. If I want it, I'll get it.

KERRY: It is at least sixteen, Rupert.

RUPERT: How does fifteen million sound?

KERRY: Yes, I am happy with that.

RUPERT: Kerry …

KERRY: Yes?

RUPERT: Are you kidding yourself that your father will agree to this?

KERRY: No, I'm not, Rupert. I will use my best endeavours to see your offer is accepted.

> *They shake hands.*

Denny Moyer has an uppercut that can break a man's jaw. Both times Mundine lost he was KO'ed. They were afraid he'd never stand again. We're going to see that up close. We're in for a good show, Rupert.

SCENE SIX

KERRY *hands something to his father in the office. The old man's eyes are nearly gone.* FRANK *turns the object in his hand.*

FRANK: No. No, what is it?

KERRY: Can't you guess?

FRANK: A rock? I can see it's a rock, a sharp rock.

KERRY: A tooth. Beaut seats, they were. Young Aboriginal middleweight, Tony Mundine, knocked it out of the old Yank's head. A full Hordern Pavilion, and it lands at my feet.

> FRANK *grins. He hands the tooth back.*

No, have it. It's for you.

> FRANK *feels the tooth in his hand.*

FRANK: You lost a bet then?

KERRY: I let Rupert Murdoch do the gambling. I got his word, Dad.

FRANK: You think he's in?

KERRY: I got a little more out of him.

FRANK: He said a price then?

KERRY: I pushed him.

FRANK: You weren't to do that. I was to talk price with him.

KERRY: I got him to fifteen million. He wants to take the *Telegraph* and *Sunday* mastheads entirely. See, I really laid it on. I said it would break your heart. To be clear, he wouldn't be getting a plant. No equipment, no building. He—

> FRANK *has a glass in his hand.*

FRANK: That's not the deal. It's not the deal. No. Now, I ordered Clyde here. Where is he?

KERRY: I'm sure he's coming.

FRANK: You telephone him.

KERRY: He's aware. He's coming. Dad, Rupert has agreed to pay all redundancies for the staff he does not take. I insisted.

FRANK: End of discussion.

KERRY: But, Dad—

FRANK: You think it's just a masthead: just typography and the columns. You don't know. I built it.

KERRY: Why would you love something that doesn't love you back?

Silence. FRANK *waves his glass.*

Clyde would appreciate you spending more time at Nine, given the challenges there.

FRANK: Come on, Temperance League lady.

KERRY *tops* FRANK's *glass.* CLYDE PACKER *launches into the room.*

CLYDE: Why couldn't this happen on the phone?

KERRY *hands his father a drink.*

FRANK: Now you listen to me, Clyde—

CLYDE: It's a dressing-down, is it? I might have guessed.

FRANK: You do not cross me, boy.

CLYDE: Kerry, leave us please.

KERRY *holds his ground.*

FRANK: Clyde, on no account is Bob Hawke to appear on Channel Nine.

CLYDE: It's that, is it? Right, well I'm amazed you even noticed; Nine has been so neglected.

KERRY: That's changing. Dad would like to spend more time at Willoughby.

CLYDE: No he wouldn't.

FRANK: Bob Hawke is a communist.

CLYDE: Look, he isn't actually.

FRANK: You're giving Hawke publicity at our expense. The ACTU has the entire nation at a standstill.

CLYDE: And the union would say McMahon is the one prolonging the crisis.

KERRY: We're with the PM on this.

CLYDE: Good. Invite him on the show. I'll let them have it, both sides, every night if need be. Balanced coverage and cracking television to boot.

FRANK: You will pull the interview.

CLYDE: I've said I can't. It's all lined up. There's nothing to replace it.

FRANK: Find something.

CLYDE: If you make me do that, you will put Michael Willesee in a position. He's signalled it already to me over censorship of his program—

FRANK: 'His' program?

CLYDE: —and I believe, when push comes to shove—he will be forced to resign. He'll quit.

FRANK: Let Willesee resign. Pull it.

CLYDE: At the cost of the most significant face of journalism in the country? I don't think so.

FRANK: He thinks journalism is all about faces now, see.

CLYDE: Actually I think it is about something far more important. You cannot use a television station like you can a newspaper to advance your own interests.

KERRY: Why not? We own it.

CLYDE: Kerry. Go to buggery, will you?

FRANK: Don't you speak to your brother like that.

CLYDE: I apologise.

KERRY: We maintain editorial control over the papers, why not Channel Nine?

FRANK: He's right. I shall have to have the show taped.

CLYDE: That's ridiculous. You mustn't. These ludicrous indulgences—

FRANK: You be careful, my boy.

CLYDE: You called the control room to have them replay your horse winning a race—

FRANK: Nonsense.

CLYDE: —for your dinner party guests. You did. It's a television network, not some personal home video device.

FRANK: I have received too many complaints about the Willesee show. All this disturbing material going over, it is quite unsuitable for seven o'clock telecasting.

CLYDE: I have addressed those complaints. That is not the issue here.

FRANK: I decided to trust you and now I have to review every second.

CLYDE: It is live. It is current affairs. It is current.

FRANK: I am spending more time at Nine. That's that. People need to know who is in charge. As for the *Telegraphs*, Clyde, you are so hell-bent on scuttling them, I think I could get twelve million.

CLYDE: Twelve? You'd never sell the *Telegraph*.

FRANK: I'm in talks with Rupert Murdoch.

CLYDE: Since when?

FRANK: You think you could get more?

CLYDE: I think twelve's a good place to pitch it, but the building alone's—

FRANK: Murdoch isn't getting the building.

CLYDE: Well, he's paid way too much.

FRANK: At twelve?

CLYDE: Yes. Gives us money to play with. It's good. Will you do it? Is that why you are saying you'll spend more time at Nine?

FRANK: Go speak to Willesee for me.

CLYDE: No, Dad, I won't.

FRANK: I am telling you to do it.

CLYDE: I understand that, but if you cost the station Willesee, the station of which I am managing director, then I will support him. I will congratulate Mike on his act of integrity.

FRANK: You are joint managing director. I own that damn station.

CLYDE: But you do not own me. You don't.

FRANK: My glass is empty.

Both sons reach for it. CLYDE *takes it.*

Kerry has been negotiating the deal with Murdoch.

CLYDE: Kerry?

FRANK: He's got Rupert to fifteen million.

CLYDE: Kerry … Well, that's how it is being played then. You've had some luck there, Kero. I wonder where you got that idea from. I'd like to see the details on the deal.

FRANK: No, I don't need you for that. You're going to go and ensure Bob Hawke and the ACTU do not appear on my station.

CLYDE: No, I am not. I believe in balance.

FRANK *laughs.*

If you make Mike Willesee walk, I'll go too. I'll quit.

FRANK: Don't be ridiculous.

CLYDE: You'd soon appreciate the efforts I make that cost me my marriage and everything else—

KERRY: Clyde, Dad's unwell. Have a drink.

CLYDE: [*ignoring* KERRY] This whole operation collapses without me.

And how will it look: your own son walking out on you?

FRANK: One flick of my pen, my boy, and you wouldn't even be that.

CLYDE: Oh, yes? Yes? Easy as that, is it? Well, go on; fire Willesee. I won't.

FRANK: Kerry will. Kerry will fire Willesee.

CLYDE: Right.

FRANK: It's done.

CLYDE: Yes. I think it is. You'll call me back, both of you, beg me back.

FRANK: You think carefully about this, Clyde.

CLYDE: Oh, I am. There is a part of my personality that I have suppressed for thirty-seven years. I'm walking. I'm walking out that door. Are you glad, are you?

FRANK: No, Clyde, you have hurt me very deeply. I have never been so ashamed in all my life. I regret all of this. You stupid boy. Go. You're fired.

CLYDE: And then … I am glad. I'm glad.

> CLYDE *exits. Silence.*

KERRY: Your drink, Dad.

> KERRY *guides his father's hand towards the glass.* FRANK*'s hand trembles.* KERRY *stills it.*

FRANK: You'll need to speak to Billy McMahon. Have them put you through. Say who you are: Sir Frank Packer's son. I can't manage the staircase at his place. Tell him to come to ours. Tonight. The PM's going to be worried about which way Rupert Murdoch leans.

> *He stands feebly with a walking stick. He puts on his hat.*

That is what you gift your competitor when you grant him this newspaper I built: a frightened prime minister on that telephone.

KERRY: I'll let Rupert know we'll proceed.

FRANK: Rupert Murdoch … he's the son I never had.

> KERRY *watches his father walk away from him.* SIR FRANK *is sore, he is slow, heavy and blind, and then he is gone.*

SCENE SEVEN

CLYDE *is in a kaftan. He stands facing* YOUNG KERRY *near their father's empty chair.*

KERRY: Christ, Clyde. You're not wearing that, are you? I've got six blokes coming in here to work through this mess.

CLYDE: I'm comfortable in this. It's a kaftan.

KERRY: I've got a suit in here; you can borrow that.

CLYDE: Already moved in, Kerry? Is he even in the crypt yet?

KERRY: Here. Put that on.

CLYDE: I haven't asked to meet with lawyers.

KERRY: Put it on please.

CLYDE: No.

KERRY: I can't have this. You look damn ridiculous.

CLYDE: Get your hands off me.

KERRY: [*wrenching up the kaftan*] Put the damn suit on, Clyde.

CLYDE: I am not. I won't. Hands off. I mean it. You might think you are managing director—

KERRY: I am managing director.

CLYDE: You may think that, but this is you and me. We are going to deal with this man to man.

KERRY: One in an evening gown.

CLYDE: We're supposed to phone the prime minister back. He'll want to express his condolences. That's something we should do together.

KERRY: I don't speak to Gough Whitlam. He ought to know that.

CLYDE: You might care to learn, Kerry.

KERRY: You heard about the bet? Les Tidmarsh was offering two to one: 'No Packer by Monday'. The old man rang him up to say he'd like a bet. You heard this?

CLYDE: Is that one true?

KERRY: Yes. It is. I was there. You weren't.

CLYDE: I patched it up with Dad. We spoke. Are you aware?

KERRY: Yes.

CLYDE: There was a codicil written to his will.

KERRY: We can't speak about this without the lawyers.

CLYDE: No, Kero, we can. We're family. They're not.

KERRY: Where are you on your plans for America?

CLYDE: I want the magazines back, Kerry. He took them from me. I am going to launch my own titles.

KERRY: Your libertarian pornos. Dad'd be disgusted.

CLYDE: Oh, Kerry—

KERRY: In my opinion it is good for you to go abroad. I think it would be better than these reports I hear about you wandering around Woollahra, walking down Queen Street, smoking marijuana.

CLYDE: Your heart's not in this, Kerry.

KERRY: Bloody disgrace.

CLYDE: Don't go talking tough to me. I know you, mate. I was with that boy who forgot his squash racket coming home from school. I remember what Dad did, how he sent you all the way back to get it. On the train, from Sydney back to Geelong.

KERRY: It was a tennis racket and you were not there; I was by myself.

CLYDE: I was there those times he took his polo whip out. And after mother died and after your accident when he really got his foot onto your throat. I stood up to him. I took him on. You never did.

KERRY: You thought you'd prove yourself essential to him, Clyde, walking away. It's only loyalty does that.

CLYDE: There was a codicil.

KERRY: I've seen it. You know you'll get a good price from me.

CLYDE: A good price? What are we talking about here?

KERRY: Alright. You've got roughly one-eighth of Consolidated. I've looked into this. I will buy out your shares. That's the simplest way.

CLYDE: I want to take charge of the magazines. You're not buying me out, shutting me out.

KERRY: I'll look after you, brother.

> KERRY *goes to a door. He undoes his belt. He sits, unseen.*

CLYDE: I'm entitled to do what I like. I did my time. My super's due.

KERRY: I'm listening.

> CLYDE *is forced to negotiate with him through the doorway.*

CLYDE: My magazines will be with other public intellectuals, artist friends. I don't intend to interfere with how you run this place.

KERRY: You can't. Don't worry. I am majority shareholder. I can require this of you. For me the simpler way forward is for you to sell, for the offer to be yours.

> *He grunts. He's taking a shit in there.*

I'd prefer this to be a very amicable arrangement. I want to look after you.

CLYDE: I can challenge this, Kerry.

KERRY: But who wants messiness, Clyde? We're a very private family. Do you really want to delight Fairfax and Murdoch? What I am laying out here is very generous.

CLYDE: Would you mind closing the door while you do it please?

The toilet roll rattles. YOUNG KERRY *is wiping his arse.*

KERRY: You see … you can do what you like over there in America, Clyde. Wear a shower curtain for all I care. You get to be the Packer that nobody knows. That's what you want, isn't it?

CLYDE: Come off it, Kero. You live in a house owned by your father. A week ago you were owned by your father.

KERRY: There is that house where you're living. Now that's in Dad's name and will be coming over to me.

CLYDE: Well that's—I am living there. It may not be in my name but it is my home.

KERRY: You're going to have the money you need for a house in America.

CLYDE: Kero … not my home.

KERRY: You can launch your new publications over in America. It's not a territory I am interested in; go for your life. I've had the lawyers draw up an agreement.

CLYDE: Four million. I won't accept less than four million.

KERRY: Let me look into that.

CLYDE: No, Kerry, you give me an answer. Right now.

The toilet flushes. KERRY *washes his hands.*

You think you can be him?

KERRY *remerges, now played by the* SENIOR PACKER *actor.*

KERRY: No. No, I think I can be better than him. You can't hack being Packer, Clyde. I can.

CLYDE: You think you can shit me out too, Kerry?

KERRY: You want to be liked. That's what Dad did to you. I don't care. I'm ugly. I've heard it all. Today is the best day of my life.

CLYDE: Four million, brother. I walk out of here. I pay my respects. I fly away.

KERRY: And it's out there, this, a very amicable separation of interests.

CLYDE: But you don't care what people think, Kerry.

KERRY: Alright, Clyde.

They shake hands.

CLYDE: The thing I know about being a tycoon, the more a person gets involved in being a tycoon, it chews up so much of him that there is less of a real person left. We're all expendable, all fallible, but tycoons believe they're not—or maybe they worry that they are. You could do the same as me: invest it, be a father, a husband. It sounds to me you're not going to do that. Well. Good luck then, Kero. Four million dollars. I don't need the Packer life for me or my son. It's a curse.

KERRY: We're done.

CLYDE: Yeah. Call Gough.

> KERRY *is alone. He moves to his father's desk. He sits in the old man's chair. He picks up the phone. He considers which number to call.*

KERRY: [*on the phone*] Yes, it's ah … it's Mister Packer here. Will you bring me a hamburger please? Yes. That's right. I'd like beetroot and cheese. Bacon. Thank you. Right away. Well, as soon as you can then. Ah, sorry, your name? Right. You'll fucking bring it right away, do you understand? Yes. Good girl.

SCENE EIGHT

The little boy in cricket whites. Thwack. He clutches his ear and wails. A cricket ball has just hurtled past him. He is LITTLE JAMIE. *A machine whirs somewhere.*

BIG KERRY *strides over, looms over him.*

KERRY: What? What? Your ear? What? Went nowhere near you. [*Calling to an unseen bowler*] False alarm. That was wide. You need to adjust it, turn it up a bit. Barry? You hear? Barry, you can up the pace? That was wide.

> BARRY KNIGHT, *former English Test cricket all-rounder, is off some distance with a pitching machine.*

[*To* JAMIE] Alright, Jamie. Turn and face.

BARRY: [*offstage, over the whir of the machine*] Is it a bit dangerous, Mister Packer?

KERRY: [*to* BARRY] No, it's good. It ought to have precise aim. It's actu-

ally a baseball machine, Barry. I have had it modified for cricket—
same company who did the World Series helmets.

BARRY: Jamie isn't wearing a helmet.

KERRY: [*to* JAMIE] I'll buy you one if you like, Jamie—if you show me
how your form has improved. Now, you listen to Mister Knight's
instructions. He is going to make something of you. [*To* BARRY] Barry,
set it at Jeff Thomson speed.

BARRY: No way, Mister Packer. Keep it safe.

KERRY: [*to* JAMIE] No no no. Grip it. Toes in line. You're not middle
stump. [*To* BARRY] Barry, is he middle stump?

BARRY: Yes.

KERRY: No he's not. [*To* JAMIE] Get to middle stump. And grip it
properly. Not too wide. Your hands. Look. They're too wide. Like
this. Like that. Take guard.

LITTLE JAMIE: What if it hits me?

KERRY: What did you say?

LITTLE JAMIE: Nothing.

KERRY: Stop the bloody grumbling. You're not going to cry, are you?

LITTLE JAMIE *shakes his head determinedly.*

[*To* BARRY] Barry, will you fix his stance? His stance is all wrong.

BARRY: He doesn't want to, Mister Packer.

KERRY: Yes he does. [*To* JAMIE] Don't you, Jamie?

LITTLE JAMIE *nods.*

BARRY: Don't make him, hey.

KERRY: [*to* BARRY] What are you trying to do: turn the boy into a wuss?

LITTLE JAMIE *positions himself bravely.*

He knows it won't hit him if his technique is correct.

BARRY: I'll bowl to him.

KERRY: No, damn it, I've got this blessed machine. I paid good money
to have it made. Are you telling me it's useless? Are you refusing me?

BARRY: In a word—

KERRY: Let's see you face it. Show him how to do it.

BARRY: No thank you. It's not safe.

KERRY: Come off it. You're one of the world's best all-rounders.

BARRY: I am the world's best all-rounder. And I am with little Jamie on
this.

KERRY: Look, do I have to show you?

BARRY: No.

KERRY: I think I do.

BARRY: No-one is asking you to do that, Mister Packer.

KERRY: Give me my bat back, Jamie. I was going to give this bat to you, son.

> KERRY *stands in the firing line. He takes his stance. The machine whirs.*

Alright, let's have it.

> *The whir. The wait.*

[*To* JAMIE] You are too bloody soft. It's your mother who's done that. When you're of age I'll be sending you to work in a salt mine, you wait.

> *He adjusts his stance, impatient for the ball.*

Jamie, this bat is a trophy and I didn't get given it for cowering like you. I was going to give it to you but you've let me down. [*To* BARRY] Christ, what's going on over there, Barry?

BARRY: I don't know.

KERRY: Pretty simple, isn't it? Drop the ball into the mechanism. It'll hurl it at me.

BARRY: Yeah …

KERRY: Well?

> *He waits.*

[*To* BARRY] Hurry up, Barry. [*To* JAMIE] I got this bat for facing my opponent head-on until they yielded.

> *He waits for the ball.*

[*To* JAMIE] There'll be no crying to mummy when you have to deal with regulators and shareholders and the International Cricket Board … Jamie, don't you forget: somebody dropped one bob and my grandfather put it on a horse and won at twelve to one. Our family started there and it could disappear just as quick.

See my grip? My—

> *Wham. The ball hits* KERRY *in the chest at breakneck speed. He emits a strange noise. He almost falls.*

[*To* BARRY] I'm alright. No. I'm alright.

He isn't alright. BARRY *races for help.*

BARRY: I'll get help.

KERRY *struggles to get his breath. He recovers. Fury rises; He smashes his bat to pieces. Spent,* KERRY *looks to the bewildered young boy.*

KERRY: [*to* JAMIE] You're fucking useless. It all ends with me.

SCENE NINE

In the vortex created by a helicopter, LITTLE JAMIE *grows to* JAMES, *aged 23. He is clutching an early, large, 1990s mobile phone on a polo field.* PARAMEDICS *and other polo* PLAYERS *whisk away* KERRY *on a stretcher.* JAMES *is left alone.*

SCENE TEN

February 1999. JAMES *is now 31.* LACHLAN MURDOCH *greets him. This is in New York.*

LACHLAN: I like your watch.
JAMES: This?
LACHLAN: I noticed it at dinner in Sydney.
JAMES: It's …
LACHLAN: How weighty is that?
JAMES: You wanna try?
LACHLAN: No that's alright. You pay too much?
JAMES: Try. Pretty weighty.
LACHLAN: I've seen these. Mine's in the shop, getting fixed.
JAMES: I did pay too much. You know they're going out of fashion?
LACHLAN: Swiss? No way.
JAMES: Watches. Everyone wants to use their phones now.
LACHLAN: Yeah? I guess we're in the right place then.
JAMES: Are you nervous?
LACHLAN: No. He's my dad. Are you?
JAMES: Lachlan, I'm a Packer. We don't feel anything, mate.
LACHLAN: How's Kerry? I heard he's unwell.
JAMES: Oh look, I'm not here to talk about that.

LACHLAN: Dad will ask.

> RUPERT MURDOCH *enters.*

RUPERT: Jamie … good to see you.

JAMES: I go by 'James' now, Rupert. Thank you for seeing me.

RUPERT: Alright, boys, at some point I have to ask this, I've got to ask this … What do we know about telephones?

LACHLAN: Okay.

JAMES: Next year starts a new century.

> *He holds up his new, small, late-90s mobile phone.*

Down there on those Manhattan streets, all those people down there like ants, pretty soon they will have news delivered to their pocket. I mean no-one can expect news will be delivered on bundles of paper in 2020.

RUPERT: Do you want a bet: my *Daily Telegraph* will be Sydney's number-one-selling news source that year?

JAMES: Maybe.

RUPERT: How much?

JAMES: Maybe. Nine News will be a contender too. One hundred percent.

RUPERT: Fancy a wager?

JAMES: I don't bet.

LACHLAN: You just helped your father buy a casino in Melbourne.

JAMES: Yeah, and a baccarat man like my father needed convincing on that. I told him the house always wins and he didn't like hearing it.

RUPERT: I heard Kerry stormed out of a board meeting over new media.

JAMES: Rupert, and as Dad says, not three percent of the stories people tell about us—

RUPERT: Are true.

JAMES: —they haven't been checked with us. I bought into One.Tel in 1995: got a loan from ANZ, off my own bat. Dad watched from the sideline and the customer growth was massive—massive; Dad couldn't be more enthusiastic now.

LACHLAN: Dad, 3G technology isn't futuristic; it's here.

RUPERT: Yeah, I know. Scrolls. We're going back to using scrolls.

JAMES: Oh, right?

RUPERT: My forecasters tell me it's like papyrus that we used to have but it lights up. Or like Moses' tablets is the other thing. It appeals to me. I could advertise on a tablet. People will, rather than freeloading on the internet. Whether a phone can do that …?

JAMES: You'll advertise on phones. They'll be your billboards, your banks and post office in your pocket. This little device is going to rule the world.

RUPERT: People will hold onto newspapers for a long time. But I know: we turned around and added 'dot com' to the name of News Corp and it put a billion dollars on the share price overnight.

JAMES *laughs.*

But y'know, I think, we built something over fifty years—eighty years—or whatever it is, and there's a strategic approach and instincts are honed—

LACHLAN: Instincts. Yes.

RUPERT: —honed over generations.

JAMES: Rupert, this is extending on what we already do—far more than our casino. This is us. It's getting in first to deliver the news in the pockets of all those ants. There is a real possibility for One.Tel to lead the Australian telecommunications industry.

RUPERT: You won't beat Telecom.

JAMES: We could be a contender.

RUPERT: They own the phone lines.

LACHLAN: This is mobiles.

RUPERT: Telecom still have the infrastructure.

LACHLAN: Telstra.

RUPERT: Telecom have the government and they have the name.

LACHLAN: It's Telstra now.

JAMES: Telstra are looking at us very closely. I know that. They're wary.

RUPERT: You won't beat them. I know that.

JAMES: You're right. We get nowhere unless we're independent. That's the ambition. Build our own network.

RUPERT: You think you can?

JAMES: I'd have to get the government to auction more spectrum. That's the network capacity the government divvies out.

RUPERT: I know what spectrum is. What are your chances?

JAMES: Ah well, if only they'd help out a media family, y'know.

RUPERT: Takes more than that.

JAMES: It does. As far as the market goes: who sells mobiles to everyday people? Mums and cabbies and to the surfers at Bondi? One.Tel is the Channel Nine and the *Daily Telegraph* of telcos.

RUPERT: They have history. They have constancy. Your grandfather's old newspaper, your father's TV network: they're both number one. You're an upstart.

LACHLAN: A start-up.

JAMES: So were they once.

RUPERT: Kerry checked into a hospital here in New York. I know that. For his heart? Or his kidneys?

JAMES: He's fine. He's good. He's back home.

RUPERT: If he's on his way out I should know.

LACHLAN: Dad?

RUPERT: Sorry, but we should know before we lock in any deals. Our thoughts are with you, Jamie.

JAMES: Kerry's good.

RUPERT: This is me asking. Can't be an easy time for the family.

JAMES: Look, Dad's never had great health. You remember that heart attack on the polo field? I mean, he was dead then for about seven minutes, stayed on his horse, y'know, and you think of the fortune he's amassed since. Dad tried relaxing, like the doctors wanted. Only once. Sold Nine to Bondy for a billion but got so bored on the boat, bought it back for a quarter of that. The Big Fella's not going anywhere.

RUPERT: I'm glad he's bounced back again.

JAMES: Yeah. Fifty billion: that's the combined market cap of Australia's telcos. Say we get third in the race. We'll be capitalised at ten billion. Got our own network. We'll go global.

RUPERT: Lachlan, I don't like how much of your time this could take.

LACHLAN: I can balance that, Dad. We're all on internet time now.

JAMES: We should also consider what happens to the share price when Lachlan and I get back to Australia. When we announce that our families back One.Tel.

RUPERT: That's not what matters. The deal matters.

JAMES: What I also meant—

RUPERT: Yes?

JAMES: Marketing muscle. Nine and News can position One.Tel.

RUPERT: 'Which Packer?' 'Which Murdoch?' They're the questions the public will ask.

JAMES: This Packer, Rupert. That Murdoch. The future.

LACHLAN: I have had a good look at this: the quality and depth of management. What we're investing in is innovators. Jodee Rich is a mastermind IT entrepreneur. Brad Keeling is a marketing genius.

RUPERT: That sounds like—

LACHLAN: PR speak. It's not.

JAMES: You'll see when you meet Jodee why he's so good.

LACHLAN: James is very enthusiastic about this guy, the culture they have at the One.Tel offices.

RUPERT: It's good. You're onto something, James. Play it right. Kerry must be proud of you.

JAMES: He said that?

RUPERT: I don't know. I won't get in the way of this succeeding for you boys.

JAMES: Right.

RUPERT: Flex the muscle. You're in charge. People need to see that. I want them to see that. Okay, I've got another meeting.

JAMES: We wanted you to meet Jodee.

LACHLAN: The innovator.

RUPERT: I have another meeting.

LACHLAN: They've flown here and—

RUPERT: I've said my piece. I trust you.

JAMES: Okay. Right. Okay.

> RUPERT *has exited.*

LACHLAN: Oh hey, here, your watch.

JAMES: No. Keep it.

SCENE ELEVEN

JAMES *approaches a hospital room.* KERRY *is comatose and wired up to hospital machinery.*

JAMES: Dad. Shit, Dad. Dad, I …

> *He takes his father's limp hand.*

Dad, I got Rupert. And I got more … Can you hear this? I wish you could hear this. Dad, I genuinely have made the decision—and it's been a very easy decision to make—that when I think of you I'm going to think great thoughts of a great man who's been incredibly generous to me. And … it has been a huge privilege to be your son.

KERRY: How long is this going to fucking take?

JAMES: Dad, how are you feeling? They managing the pain?

KERRY: They have me so full of … making me 'comfortable' but … won't bring me fucking Coca-Cola with crushed fucking ice when I ask.

JAMES: I'll get that. I'll get you that. Don't worry. You relax.

KERRY: Fucking … I'm fucking fading, son.

JAMES: Yeah, you're … You know I'm ready. You know that.

KERRY: You, you carve your own path.

JAMES: Yep. Yeah. Things have fallen into place, Dad. Things have … I've landed something.

KERRY: Rupert …

JAMES: Yeah, I'm just back from New York. Something more though. Something massive and … I want you to know—

KERRY: I want Coca-Cola. Crushed ice.

JAMES: Yeah, I will … You relax. You can relax. Are you allowed cola?

KERRY: I want it—I fucking want it.

JAMES: Yeah. Yep. I'll ask someone. But, Dad, listen, this is big for us. The One.Tel deal with the Murdochs, it has triggered something much more—Telstra have got their acquisitions team all over me. This is huge—

KERRY: They keep sending these shirt-lifter nurses in here. See if you can lay down some ground rules: only good sorts in short skirts.

JAMES: Dad, are you listening to me?

KERRY: If Telstra want One.Tel, you fucking bleed them, son.

JAMES: I am. But not just One.Tel. Telstra's offer is for the lot. They've made an offer for all of us: all of PBL. Phones, TV, magazines. Convergence. It's a new century and they get it. They're not idiots, not fucking idiots.

KERRY: What are you on about?

JAMES: The multiple is insane. They're offering—

KERRY: What are they offering?

JAMES: They're offering sixteen dollars a share, Dad.

KERRY: Unbelievable.

JAMES: We keep the private holdings. They take all media assets.

KERRY: Christ, son, you're more Packer than Packer. You want to sell up?

JAMES: I am promising you, Dad, that I couldn't look myself in the mirror if I felt I was a leech on what you built and my grandfather built. One.Tel might have opened this door but everything you instilled lives on and … I don't wanna cry. Shit.

KERRY: Telstra is partially government owned. PBL's got a fucking casino.

JAMES: Telstra carve out Crown Resorts, sell it back to us below what it's worth. The deal is good. The price is undeniably massive. Massive. The casino's there in Melbourne, always there for me, just to make money—but media is our bloodline and I'll re-enter the new media. A downturn's gonna come and I'll want full pockets. Because broadcast TV's gonna face huge challenges but Telstra want it all for sixteen a share. Sixteen. Funny thing is, right now, it's me who's proud, Dad—of you. I love you. I love you, Dad.

KERRY: You know, son, you need to hear this …

JAMES: Yes, Dad?

KERRY: I'll be dead soon—

JAMES: Don't say that.

KERRY: —and you can do what you like. You won't have to wait long.

JAMES: Surely there's some way we can pay for a kidney. Bend the rules. Try in South America or Asia. Whatever the cost. Fuck.

KERRY: Calm down. I am not strong enough for the operation. If this sale is what you want to do, what you think is right, you have my blessing.

JAMES: Thank you, Dad. I love you.

KERRY: But at eighteen dollars a share. Show them you are willing to walk.

JAMES: I've got this deal cemented. Sixteen is—

KERRY: No no. Push them to eighteen.

JAMES: Dad, I've pushed.

KERRY: Trust me. Don't be a fool falling for the first glittering fucking thing they put in front of you.

JAMES: My instincts are for sixteen.

KERRY: —

JAMES: Are you sure? You're sure …

KERRY: So long as I'm alive you'll kick that price up for me, son. Eighteen or walk away.

JAMES: Right … I'll do it, for you, Dad. I'll get you eighteen.

KERRY: You'll see. You'll see, son. Now, one of those pretty little nurses is due to give me a sponge bath. You're welcome to watch or be on your way.

JAMES: Yeah. Yeah, alright. Got some calls to make but, um, I'm not far. I … I love you.

KERRY: And I love you, son.

> JAMES *leaves. Pause.* KERRY *claws himself to the edge of the bed. He reaches for the cannula. He eases it from his veins.*
>
> *Blood oozes. He disentangles himself from the medical apparatus. He stands in his hospital gown, whoozy.*
>
> *A camp male* NURSE *arrives with a tub and sponges.*

NURSE: Now what's this, mister? No no no, back in that bed, thank you muchly.

KERRY: Fuck off, cunt. I want Coca-Cola with crushed ice. No-one is bringing it, so I am going to get it my fucking self.

> KERRY *strides out, arse exposed, trailing blood.*

END OF ACT ONE

ACT TWO

SCENE ONE

The Arctic P *is a converted icebreaker and leisure vessel.* JAMES PACKER *lounges inside in a large T-shirt and Speedos.* JODEE RICH *is in rich-man boat-wear beside him.*

JODEE: I'd have to say, yeah, for me, it is that. I mean, y'know, look at it out there. In the mornings I kayak in on all that. I just rest my kayak against the sandstone at Mrs Macquarie's Chair, round there. Walk up through the gardens, through the CBD. And that's just my commute. That's happiness. This city. That body of water.

JAMES: Anyone ever flog y'kayak?

JODEE: I think I could afford to replace it. And, really, I'm not driven by money.

JAMES: That's easy to say.

JODEE: What excites me is that we created something.

JAMES: You did, Jodee. I just backed you.

JODEE: Tell me you are stopping to enjoy this, James.

JAMES: I'm on the harbour, aren't I?

> JAMES *reaches for his laptop which has a trail of cords leading to an internet device.*

JODEE: I just checked it. Still no more bids from Hutchinson. Or Primus.

JAMES: If we lose reception the skipper can shift us closer to Rose Bay.

JODEE: Why aren't you enjoying this?

JAMES: Mate. I am. Dad's just very pessimistic about the spectrum auction.

JODEE: Is Kerry coming aboard today?

JAMES: Nah. Been a bit under the weather.

JODEE: Why be pessimistic? That's what I'd like to ask him.

JAMES: Don't.

JODEE: The government gave us this auction. Gave it to you, James.

JAMES: Pessimism has served him well.

JODEE: Has it ever served you?

JAMES: Nepotism has served me.

JODEE: What do you want me to say to that?

JAMES: To what?

JODEE: You, prodding with these little self-deprecating—these things I hear you say. Even at board level there are these, these, stabs, self-inflicted and—

JAMES: I'm not asking you to say anything.

JODEE: Yes you are. You're the most numerically brilliant person I have ever met. You have remarkable foresight. You have the best instincts I've seen in business and you're a kind, loyal person. There, well, I did say it. Just like you wanted.

JAMES: I have this feeling …

JODEE: Yeah?

JAMES: I have this feeling Telstra will to do everything to screw us.

JODEE: James. James, Telstra are not even in this auction.

JAMES: They're gonna bleed us on price. The Telstra board hate that they failed to buy us.

JODEE: That takeover falling through was the best day of our lives. Thank God you had the balls to push them to eighteen. That took guts.

JAMES: Yeah.

JODEE: And look where your big balls got us. We're about to get our own network then Europe then the US and the rest. We'll collect a founder's bonus: that's how high the share price is headed, especially after this auction. We're going to show them. You know why?

JAMES: Yeah. Luck. Strategy. Numbers.

JODEE: Because you walked into the bloody telecommunication minister's office—and you were on the phone to the prime minister. I saw that. Your father didn't see that. You got us this second spectrum auction.

JAMES: Yeah, well … Still keeps me up at night. Without the spectrum we can't use the network we're building. We have to win this auction and I don't know if Dad will refuse to get his purse out.

JODEE: Have you tried magnesium for sleeping?

JAMES: No.

JODEE: You should. Without a proper balance of magnesium to other minerals like calcium, a heart attack can happen because of severe muscle spasms. I'm talking down the track. At your age it's more about a restful sleep.

JAMES: Okay. I will.

JODEE: James, I hear you: there are risks. The numbers are good, we've got clout with lenders if we need it. I'm not ignoring the situation. You've got to keep an eye on what matters, why we do it. What's *your* pinnacle? What does good feel like for James? That's what I wanna know. Honestly.

JAMES: A packet of Dunhills.

JODEE: James?

JAMES: You said be honest, Jodee. Ciggis. Bit of time to smoke them.

JODEE: Got any?

JAMES: You don't smoke.

JODEE: I would with you.

JAMES: Nah, I'm off the durries. Yeah. Dad says our rivals are big gorillas and they're going to fuck us.

JODEE: James, one of these days you're going to have to deny your father.

Silence.

JAMES: There's a thing you get in Capri. This chocolate, like—it has a layer— a shell layer of chocolate. I'm not explaining it very well.

JODEE: Yes you are.

JAMES: It's just, the ice cream inside is very hard, like deep frozen. We ate this thing out in the square where people—

JODEE: You and your wife?

JAMES: Yeah. Where people all just hang out. No-one knows you. My fiancée—my ex. Yeah. In Capri. I don't know what it's called, the dessert. The way the chocolate cracks and ... Dunno.

JODEE: Sounds nice.

JAMES: Yeah, just being in the square with ... The Leopard we had from Benetti marina wasn't a half-bad dinghy either, and I think that day was, y'know, maximum happiness, real and like ...

Silence.

Have you logged on? [*The laptop*] It's loading.

JODEE: My wife and I are getting a helicopter to fly us into the Himalayas. They land you there and you're in your skiing gear with—

JAMES: I'm on. We're good, Jodee. No bids.

JODEE: What'd I say? This auction is ours.

JAMES: Those doubters. [*To his laptop, about the auction*] Eat my shorts. Eat my shorts.

> JODEE *wrestles with him.*

What are you? [*Laughing*] Mad, fuckin' mad bastard.

JODEE: Come on. Wrestle me.

> KERRY PACKER *is behind them at the door.*

Wrestle me.

JAMES: Ha. You fuckwit. Ha ha.

JODEE: Who's the gorilla now?

KERRY: What the fuck are you two doing? What is this?

JAMES: No, we were just—

KERRY: What? What?

JAMES: Wrestling.

KERRY: Rolling around like a couple of retarded children?

JAMES: Yes.

KERRY: You were?

JAMES: No.

KERRY: Primus are in with a bid.

JAMES: Primus?

JODEE: Hutchinson, I think you mean. Tested the water at the start. Meaningless.

KERRY: No, son, I mean what I fucking say. A little birdie phoned the house. Primus will outbid Hutchinson.

JAMES: Primus? When?

KERRY: I thought you preschoolers were in here watching this thing.

JAMES: Look, Dad, we knew this might happen—

KERRY: Bullshit you did. Bullshit.

JAMES: I mean, I know, but—

KERRY: They gave me this auction. We're going to win it. You need more coin. You need to outbid them.

JAMES: You'll let me? What are they at?

KERRY: Two fifty mil.

JODEE: Shit. Big jump.

JAMES: You'll let me spend? Can we outbid?

KERRY: Howard won't give me another auction, son. You're building a network that will be redundant. D'you believe in this?

JAMES: Of course I do. Do you?

KERRY: Put in another bid.

JAMES: Another ten.

KERRY: Ten?

JAMES: More?

KERRY: I hope you don't enjoy being fucked by gorillas, son. That'd be a burden for your old man.

JAMES: Right. More. Twenty.

JODEE: [*offering somewhere to sit*] Would you like a chair, Mister Packer?

KERRY: What?

JODEE: Just thought—

KERRY: Thought what? I was about to die?

JODEE: No I—

KERRY: These are my chairs—it's my boat—don't go offering my fucking chairs—

JODEE: Sure. No problem.

KERRY: Well, there is a problem. You're being fucked.

JODEE: No no. We're in a very dominant position—

KERRY: What have you been smoking, son?

JODEE: With the share price in the billions we can get the finance. And James, the deals he struck, the way government yield to him, a lotta love for James. He's right to be proud. Don't you think, Mister Packer? You've gotta love him. Got to—

JAMES: Jodee, it's alright. Don't.

KERRY: What are you getting at?

JAMES: Dad, let's take it to two-eighty million. I'll call Bankers Trust. My relationship is solid there. Let's show them who's the gorilla.

JODEE: This guy. A lotta love for this guy.

KERRY: Rich, give me a moment with my son, will you? I want to lavish him with praise and lord knows how self-conscious I get.

JODEE: Oh. Yes. I'll call into HQ. I'll …

    JODEE *exits*.

KERRY: You're going to hit up Lachlan and Rupert for more coin. We'll match what they toss in. Borrow the rest.

JAMES: I'm pleased you believe in this. I'll speak to the Murdochs.

KERRY: And when Jodee comes back, I want you to sack him.

JAMES: What?

KERRY: You'll do it.

JAMES: Dad. He is One.Tel.

KERRY: I am fucking One.Tel. Read the paper. I am One.Tel. I am the reason Murdoch wanted in and the reason he'll sign your next cheque. I am the reason the communications minister offered this spectrum auction. I am the reason Howard wants you to succeed. Jodee Rich is gone. Do it.

JAMES: Well, there would have to be a board meeting.

KERRY: Bullshit. Who's in charge of our investment? Him?

JODEE *knocks on the door.*

JAMES: Come in.

JODEE *enters.*

JODEE: Sorry to …

KERRY: What is it?

JODEE: Not the best news I'm afraid. SMS's coming through now. There's been a bit of a flurry.

KERRY: I can hear gorillas. Is that right, Rich? Are they gang-banging you and my son?

JODEE: The bids are near five hundred million. They're trying to crush us. What do we do?

KERRY: James? What do we do?

JAMES: Jodee, I got in on this from the start because I believe in One.Tel. This is how we take my family's business into the new era. I'm going to the PBL directors to authorise that we lead the capital raising to win this auction. I will ask Rupert and Lachlan to do the same.

KERRY: There are a few things necessary for the workable future of One. Tel.

JAMES: Yeah. And Jodee …

JODEE: Yes, James.

JAMES: When I back an idea, I don't give it a little tap to see if it stands up. I back it all the way. And I back people I believe in. You have my full support, Jodee. That needs to be said.

JODEE: I appreciate that, James. [*Nodding thanks to* KERRY] Mister Packer.

SCENE TWO

A computer and modem are set up on KERRY'*s desk by* DANIEL, *an executive.* JAMES *is with a scrum of* MALE EXECUTIVES.

JAMES: Fellas, right now, we are on top. We're winning—and we can't rest, okay. Today is to show Dad—there's a demo we're gonna run. Daniel's made it look—I think it looks excellent—to show Dad where we are in the tech space. Because, y'know, some of the old blokes think an email costs forty-five cents.

> *The* MEN *laugh at* JAMES'*joke.* JAMES *laughs too. PBL finance director,* NICK FALLOON, *does not laugh.*

[We'll] See Dad fuckin' licking this computer screen if we're not careful. Y'know to send an email. Nah, but really—

> KERRY *arrives. The laughter halts.* KERRY *is in comfortable clothes, holding a golf club.* JAMES *kisses* KERRY *hello.*

Hello, Dad.

KERRY: What am I supposed to be looking at?

JAMES: We'll start.

> DANIEL *is at the computer.*

DANIEL: We're just waiting for it to …

JAMES: Fellas, what Daniel will show you here is what we're doing with Microsoft. We've spoken about future-proofing. So, instead of just websites for our magazines, we take the experience online—

KERRY: Who reads magazines on a computer?

JAMES: Yeah, no, fair enough. They will.

KERRY: You are wasting your time. Nobody wants to sit around all day looking at tiny fucking screens.

JAMES: But the deal. Let's just. We are essentially getting the portal and other products for free.

KERRY: Son, nothing is fucking free.

> *The* MEN *laugh at* KERRY'*s remark.* JAMES *laughs too.*

JAMES: Fair cop. Fair cop.

KERRY: I ought to fucking know. What is it costing me to have all these bastards standing around doing nothing?

JAMES *hands* KERRY *a paper report.*

JAMES: We don't want to weigh you blokes down with paper reports so PDFs have been emailed to you all.

DANIEL: We get Microsoft's portal. That's the crux.

JAMES: [*for* KERRY] The portal is the internet interface providing links to other sites.

DANIEL: Like a gateway.

KERRY: A portal is like a gateway. Oh, brave new world.

The MEN *laugh.*

JAMES: Internet Explorer in Australia will open automatically to our website. ninemsn is the gateway.

DANIEL: It's how users get to Hotmail, for example.

JAMES: The free email service, Dad. It is free, actually.

He laughs a little, but laughs alone.

It's great for us because all those eyeballs and clicks come through the ninemsn frame: our banner ads, our content.

KERRY *kicks off his shoes and puts his feet up on the desk.*

KERRY: We still waiting, Daniel?

DANIEL: No, it's just the …

JAMES: Is it because of the dial-up or …?

DANIEL: It's because—yeah.

JAMES: Do you think maybe reboot?

DANIEL: No, I think … [*Indicating the screen*] Mister Packer, you see the clock turn there?

KERRY: No.

DANIEL: There.

KERRY: Yes.

DANIEL: That means it is thinking.

KERRY: Scintillating. Who saw my horse win on the weekend?

The other MEN *respond that they saw his horse win.*

It's all in the breeding. We knew she would be a winner two generations back. Otherwise I would have had her shot.

JAMES: We can find it on here. We'll be able to find Dad's horse winning on ninemsn.

DANIEL: Can we?

JAMES: [*to* DANIEL] Like a clip from the news.

DANIEL: [*to* JAMES] Video? Not yet.

KERRY: It's in the newspaper. Hand me that.

JAMES: We'll just wait for that to … But, headline is, creating ninemsn has led to an opportunity with eBay. Which is big.

KERRY: [*to an* EMPLOYEE] You. Go and see if my secretary has some fucking cake for me. [*To another* EMPLOYEE] You, find my horse winning in there.

KERRY *tosses the newspaper to* EMPLOYEE 2. *It comes apart.*

JAMES: The online auction site caused a sensation—you guys know this. eBay grew from a shed in a whizkid's backyard in San Francisco.

KERRY: Nick Falloon. Please tell me the truth, Nick. I don't believe anything these young blokes tell me.

NICK FALLOON: eBay is at US nine billion on Nasdaq.

KERRY: Nasdaq? Nasdaq? There is so much hot air over there. It's a fart. Back me up, Nick. A fart.

NICK FALLOON: I agree there is over speculation on the US technology market.

KERRY: Yes. A hot one.

NICK FALLOON: But, it would be extraordinary to get the national eBay franchise gratis.

KERRY: Let's stop fucking confusing this. It is not for free. I don't want to put any more money into this internet side of the business.

JAMES: Nick, what is our estimated market cap for that side of the business?

NICK FALLOON: For ecorp? Oh look, it's …

JAMES: What is it, conservatively?

NICK FALLOON: Yeah, it's a lot.

JAMES: You think seven hundred million?

KERRY: Turn it up, son.

NICK FALLOON: Or plus that but—

KERRY: It's just a list of websites. These inflated prices we are seeing are nothing but guesswork.

JAMES *moves.*

I saw that. Don't you fucking shrug like that in here, James.

JAMES: I didn't. Sorry.

KERRY: If consuming cash and not making profit is how you do business, then I am a Dutchman.

JAMES: The shareholders disagree.

KERRY: With me?

EMPLOYEE 1 *returns with some fruitcake.*

JAMES: The board are also very excited about this.

KERRY: And I don't think boards matter a damn as long as they don't do anything.

EMPLOYEE 2, *who was tossed the newspaper, can't find* KERRY'*s horse. He gets help from another of the* MEN.

You think you're gazing at the future, but where are the companies of substance that make and do anything in all this?

KERRY *eats the cake.*

JAMES: Let's just focus on the—

KERRY: This isn't fucking cake; it's shit. I'm a sick man. She's feeding me a man's shit. Where'd she get it? The lav?

EMPLOYEE 1: She said she bought it from David Jones Food Hall.

KERRY: Well, tell her to take it fucking back. I'll have to go on dialysis again to flush that crap out of me.

He tips the cake off his desk with his golf club.

Go get me some fucking rocky road.

EMPLOYEE 1 *hurries away with the bits of cake in his hands.*

Now, tell me, what on earth are we doing here? You boys in long shorts have called us here and there is no fucking show. I want my office back.

EMPLOYEE 2: There's your …

KERRY: What?

EMPLOYEE 2: Your horse, Mister Packer. [*Then*] Tumble On looks good at Randwick on Saturday.

KERRY: Thank you very much. I appreciate that, son. You like a flutter?

JAMES: Dad, I just want to say—

KERRY: What? What do you want to say? I wish you would make fuck-ing sense to me, James.

JAMES: We'll be eating the dust of our competitors. Fairfax could dominate digital. Seven and News Limited are already converging 'infotainment'. What I've got over them is a one-stop media shop: email, news, eventually watch a TV show, and while you're there you make purchases on eBay. Add my acquisitions of the leading Car Sales website and job ads: a site called Seek. I'm pursuing exactly what my grandfather was chasing: the rival's classifieds. Plus we have further integration ahead as a phone and internet provider.

KERRY: Nick. Speak up, Nick, will you? I have veto over these things; I like to hear from people who share my old-fashioned scepticism.

NICK FALLOON: I agree with James to a large extent.

KERRY: Why would you do a thing like that?

NICK FALLOON: I don't quite share your faith in One.Tel, if I can just say that, James.

JAMES: You're entitled to your view, Nick. It's important that you speak.

KERRY: One.Tel has terrific potential. I wouldn't be in One.Tel otherwise. However, it is currently run by cretins.

NICK FALLOON: Management is my concern too.

JAMES: If we can just keep our focus—

KERRY: Go on, Nick. We need to kick a few heads in, do we?

NICK FALLOON: In a way.

JAMES: Look, we don't actually.

NICK FALLOON: We are all using One.Tel mobiles and the coverage is terrible, customer service is a joke—

JAMES: Well try our competitors. It's a brand new market. It's very fluid. Jodee's very open about that.

NICK FALLOON: The reporting is confusing.

JAMES: That's a purpose-built billing system. Jodee and I take a lot of pride in it.

KERRY: Daniel.

DANIEL: Yep.

KERRY: Is this going to take all fucking week?

DANIEL: Yeah, no, I'm rebooting.

KERRY: Because some of us have church on Sunday.

The MEN *laugh with* KERRY. *He hands a fat wad of cash to* EMPLOYEE 2.

There you are, son. Put it on a pony.

JAMES: Look, there were doubters when I said One.Tel would break through. There is no arguing with the share price. As soon as we complete the European network, it will skyrocket.

KERRY: Says who? Jodee Rich?

JAMES: Murdoch. Murdoch is saying that.

KERRY: Rupert can spend and say what he likes. I refuse to pour more into One.Tel when Jodee Roach and his mates just paid themselves sixty-two million.

JAMES: Really that is how fast things can move, you know, that One. Tel's founders can reap rewards at warp speed. I actually think it is fantastic.

KERRY: Do you?

JAMES: Yes. And, Nick, I can tell you that I've never been more convinced of One.Tel's success. A company four years old is suddenly worth more than one eighty years in the making.

KERRY: Which company?

JAMES: One.Tel's share price is higher than PBL. It's valued at more than our entire—

KERRY: Where? On your fucking computer? Well, go on, cash in your hologram money, Boy Jetson.

DANIEL: Oh, here we are.

The computer is finally ready.

Oop. Has it frozen?

KERRY: Are you mentally deficient? When I switch on my television it comes on straight away. When you get it fucking working, you give me a fucking call. [*To the* MEN] Now, you lot, stop all this arse scratching and do some fucking work.

JAMES: Okay, thanks for coming, guys. If we can just say—it doesn't matter the demo hasn't worked; you all know what a computer does but, ah—there is a significant opportunity here. It would be remiss not to seize it. We'll be moving on the eBay deal. And ninemsn goes live as a matter of urgent priority. Thanks, Nick. Thanks, everyone.

The EXECUTIVES *leave, muttering thanks to* JAMES. DANIEL *hurries to shut down the computer and unplug the cords.*

Dad, I cannot be—

KERRY: Take your hands out of your pockets. You treat this place like a fucking ski lodge: joking about with your fucking schoolmates. Where does Jodee Rich's sixty-two million come from?

JAMES: That is One.Tel's return of capital. He shares some of it. It's in his contract.

KERRY: No, it is money invested by me and fucking Rupert.

DANIEL *races to free his computer and modem from the sockets and bundle it. He scurries away, the mouse banging along after him as* EMPLOYEE 1, *the rocky road man, returns but quickly exits.*

JAMES: Jodee's entitled to the payment. He's a founding shareholder. He is the founder.

KERRY: Like you? Because you won't be taking money out, James. It belongs to me.

JAMES: I ... Dad, this is profit made from my original investment in One.Tel.

KERRY: No, how you see it is wrong, plain wrong. You don't have your money.

JAMES: I backed this with a loan from ANZ. Really, it is distinct from any family companies.

KERRY: You only get a loan because you are Packer's son. You can't swim without my capital. You don't exist in business without me.

JAMES: Yes, Dad.

KERRY: I want full reports—not his senseless projections. Raw data—give me that without Jodee's crayons all over it. Personally, I wouldn't hire Jodee Rich as a sweeper. You seem to think he is some sort of guru. Why is that?

JAMES: I believe in him. I respect him.

KERRY: Don't be wet. You'll put your One.Tel bonus back into the family holdings. It's not your money.

JAMES: Dad ...

KERRY: Fair is fair, son.

JAMES: Alright. Fine. I see the family companies as me anyway. But lay off Jodee. We need him.

KERRY: I don't.

JAMES: I do.

KERRY: Why? I just don't understand it.

JAMES: He's a friend.

KERRY: Get a dog.

JAMES: I share his vision. He values me. He values me.

KERRY: I always knew about you, Jamie. You're a complete fucking wuss.

JAMES: I see him as my ticket to not needing your money anymore. Jodee and One.Tel buy me my independence. I am about to be a billionaire in my own right. You know that now and it is killing you.

> KERRY *is speechless. He uses the golf club to hoist himself up and then as a kind of walking stick.*

KERRY: Those reports are to be delivered to my hospital room every day.

JAMES: Hospital?

KERRY: Yes, I just came from there.

JAMES: Weren't you on the golf course?

KERRY: Let people think that. I'm going under the knife, but—

JAMES: Sorry, Dad, I didn't know. What's the operation?

KERRY: Transplant.

JAMES: You found a donor? Who?

KERRY: My chopper pilot. Biggles.

JAMES: He'll give you his kidney?

KERRY: I don't like talking about it. It's … it's not a monetary thing. He's not asking for that. They'd never allow that if he did. And … that a man would do that for me … it's …

JAMES: I'd like to be there. I'll be there. I love you. You know I love you.

> JAMES *and* KERRY *don't see* EMPLOYEE 1 *leave the plate and scram.*

KERRY: Just deliver me the reports.

JAMES: Dad …

KERRY: Son, I can run this fucking company from the grave if I have to.

> KERRY *exits with his golf club as a walking stick.* JAMES *is left at his father's desk.*

SCENE THREE

KERRY *is under a sheet.* DOCTOR BOB WRIGHT *shines a light in his eyes.*
JAMES *enters.*

JAMES: Oh good, is he …?
BOB WRIGHT: Out of it. The operation was the easy part. Now we're in
the danger zone. What's that?

> JAMES *has a file in his hand.*

You're not leaving that for him, are you?
JAMES: He said—
BOB WRIGHT: No. It's a work document.
JAMES: Fine. It's fine. Better to just … Let him rest. That's fine.
BOB WRIGHT: And you stop his associates coming to the ward. This is
touch and go. I'm serious.
JAMES: Right. I know. Yep.
KERRY: Am I dead?
JAMES: Shit.
BOB WRIGHT: Very sleepy. The painkillers have you in and out.
KERRY: I feel dead.
BOB WRIGHT: Kerry, your body is rejecting the new kidney.
KERRY: Bob … would ya pop down and grab me a Fanta please?
BOB WRIGHT: No, I'm not doing that. You've had an organ transplant.
You need to rest.
KERRY: Rest? I can hardly fucking move.
BOB WRIGHT: That has its advantages.
KERRY: James is here, is he?
JAMES: Um. Yes, Dad.
KERRY: You bring it?
BOB WRIGHT: No he didn't—
JAMES: Jodee is outside. Some things to explain.

> JAMES *hands* KERRY *the report.*

KERRY: Pass me my reading glasses.
BOB WRIGHT: No, come on, hand it here.
KERRY: What things, James?

BOB WRIGHT: Honestly, you have to follow my orders now, Kerry. I'm in charge. You hear?

JAMES: Now, Dad—

KERRY: Shit. This is the Nasdaq?

JAMES: Just some—

KERRY: Whack the telly on.

BOB WRIGHT: No. Stop. No.

JAMES: Dad, listen first—

KERRY: Rich! Get fucking Rich in here.

BOB WRIGHT: Look, I'm really putting my foot down.

KERRY: Don't make me fucking charge at that door, Bob.

BOB WRIGHT: You might die if you do that.

KERRY: Rich! Get in here, Rich!

JAMES: I'll get him.

KERRY: You stay right there. Rich!

BOB WRIGHT: Fine. Fine with me. I get a bequest when you're dead.

> KERRY *sizes him up, then laughs.*

KERRY: You're alright, son. You win.

BOB WRIGHT: Good. Now close your eyes. You're very heavily—

> JODEE *enters, in lycra with kneepads.*

JODEE: Hiya. Hi, all.

BOB WRIGHT: Ah, okay, thanks, he's resting.

KERRY: Rich, you little prick, you're going to run out of cash.

JODEE: That is simply not true, Kerry. There is revenue in the pipeline. This is just some volatility.

BOB WRIGHT: I really must insist—

JAMES: All the dot.coms are experiencing this contraction—

KERRY: Because they are speculative pieces of shit. I was right and now the markets are with me.

JAMES: We're still making money.

KERRY: Are you? You haven't met your projections. You're burning cash.

> KERRY *tries to turn.*

JAMES: Aw, Dad, we can see what you had for breakfast.

KERRY: Sausages and mash. Take a seat, Rich. Go on, sunshine, pull up a commode. I have questions. One question. How much cash does One.Tel have?

BOB WRIGHT: No. Stop. Please. Really.

KERRY: [*to* BOB] But look at me, doc; I am feeling better already.

JODEE: We forecast we will have seventy-five million in cash at the end of the year.

JAMES: Jodee, you need to explain to Dad how you can make that promise.

BOB WRIGHT *remains. He sits patiently.*

JODEE: You know, I spent a lot of time in California and particularly in San Francisco. There's a culture there around innovation which is start-ups need to be nurtured, not threatened.

KERRY *has now dozed off.*

Is he?

BOB WRIGHT: Finally.

JODEE: Should we …?

BOB WRIGHT: Yes please. Out. He's very heavily medicated.

KERRY: [*unaware of his micro-sleep*] The crash is on, son. Nasdaq's just the first fucking teeter. What are you going to fucking change?

JAMES: We are launching a Next Generation Mobile Network. We are undercutting our local calls to lure customers from Telstra to our profitable long distance calls. Jodee?

KERRY *drifts momentarily.*

JODEE: That's right, James. And at the forefront of my mind is: Macquarie Bank endorse us as a three-point-five-billion dollar company so …

They all check if KERRY *is lucid. He isn't.*

KERRY: [*seemingly still asleep*] Where is Nick Falloon? He mans up on this.

JAMES: No, Dad, I've … Nick has moved on. I let him go.

KERRY: Why?

JAMES: We can talk about it in private. A head had to roll: the ratings at Nine.

KERRY: You chose Nick?

JAMES: I needed a batsman, not a wicketkeeper. Broadcast TV isn't what it was.

KERRY: I have these fucking mood swings. It's these fucking anti-rejection drugs. [*To* BOB] Is that what it is, Bob?

BOB WRIGHT: What do you care what I think?

KERRY: [*to* JAMES *and* JODEE] I sometimes have unexplained bouts of cheerfulness. I apologise for the mixed messages. I want to be clear. You are doing a fucking terrible job at One.Tel. Clearly you are both fucking imbeciles. I am sending some blokes in to kick the tyres.

JODEE: Okay, look, you seem pretty cranky. I sense that.

KERRY: You sense my thumb up your arse?

JODEE: No I ... Kerry, we have an extraordinarily flat structure—I know that is the antithesis to how you work, but this is One.Tel.

KERRY: 'Mister Packer'.

JODEE: Yes.

KERRY: You call me that.

JODEE: Mister Packer. We have an extraordinary management team in a very, very competitive industry.

KERRY: Jesus, son, what the fuck are you wearing?

JODEE *is wearing lycra bike shorts.*

JODEE: I'm sorry. I was on my way somewhere when I got the call to be here. I was rollerblading.

JAMES: Jodee, Dad needs full reports. We need to see all that you're promising.

JODEE: But James, your father has been involved in every important decision that goes on at One.Tel. The message I have received from PBL is that you are delighted with the number of subscribers that we're adding, the profitability. Are you telling me something different now, Mister Packer? James?

KERRY: Alright, I have listened to you, son, now you can fucking well listen to me. I can see your share price plummeting and no-one can give me a true cash position or the extent of the debt and I have my helicopter pilot's kidney trying to crawl out my Jap's eye, so don't you ask me if I am a bit cranky; I am fucking furious.

JAMES: Okay. Look, we have to stick to our strategy, right. We have spent five hundred million on spectrum.

KERRY: You fucked up. You paid gallons more than your competitors. And ... you ...

KERRY *nods off.*

JODEE: He told us to do that. He urged us into that auction.

JAMES: What are you—? Don't talk back.

JODEE: He's asleep.

JAMES: So?

KERRY: … didn't buy enough spectrum and … What? Jodee? What did you say to me?

JAMES: I'm just saying that there is a new climate and we're being challenged in the race. But we know what we are creating: a telco in a very competitive market.

JODEE: You got us there, Mister Packer. Kerry Packer is One.Tel. We're proud of that.

KERRY: When I want my balls tongued I book a bordello. Get me out of bed. [*To* BOB] Bob, I want to sit at the window.

BOB WRIGHT: You can't.

KERRY: I need my blokes to gather around me. I'm hungry, Bob. Will you send one of the girls down to the cafeteria? A couple of Violet Crumbles please. I want to sit up.

BOB WRIGHT: Wait, I'll get the team.

KERRY: [*as he presses a call button*] Get me over to the window and we'll bash about a few strategies.

JODEE: We know our strategy. We need to raise more capital.

JAMES: Jodee—

KERRY: [*to* JODEE] Jodee, I can assure you, this will cost you your right testicle.

JODEE: What does that actually mean?

JAMES: Jodee, go wait in the corridor, mate.

JODEE: Right?

JAMES: You and me need to have a chat; I'll find you.

JODEE: Sure. Alright then.

> JODEE *exits.*

JAMES: Now, Dad—

> KERRY *struggles to move. He can't. He's in pain.*

KERRY: Fuck. Fuck it. Fuck, I need to move.

> JAMES *offers his hand.*

JAMES: Here.

KERRY: Help.

JAMES: I am.

BOB WRIGHT: Careful.

KERRY: Fuck.

BOB WRIGHT: Careful.

JAMES: Take it easy. Are you alright?

KERRY: No I'm not.

JAMES: We can correct the slide. We have to remain committed.

KERRY: Ahh, I'm bleeding. Where's this blood coming from?

BOB WRIGHT: I said to wait. You have to wait. You've snagged the catheter. That must be very painful.

KERRY: No.

BOB WRIGHT: You've made a tear; you've tugged the entry point. It's gaping. Very raw.

> KERRY *laughs.*

KERRY: James.

BOB WRIGHT: Just lie back. The pain is overwhelming. Is it?

KERRY: I said it was … … all just hot …

> *He cocks his leg, feebly, to fart.*

BOB WRIGHT: Don't, don't break wind, you could rupture something. I'll get this cleaned up.

KERRY: Stupid young bastards love telling us what to do.

BOB WRIGHT: We have to guard against infection.

JAMES: I wanna fly over and see the Murdochs in person. I am going to—I can correct this.

BOB WRIGHT: Rest back, Kerry. Rest.

> KERRY *is drifting off again.*

JAMES: Doc, you're to give me full reports on his state. I'll be in the air but I can be reached via my office day or night. He's drifting. He's drifting off now.

SCENE FOUR

JODEE, JAMES *and* LAWYERS *convene in One.Tel's headquarters.*

Meanwhile, LACHLAN MURDOCH *is at a speaker phone in New York, communicating with his Sydney colleagues.*

JAMES: You still with us there, Lachlan?

Silence.

LACHLAN: I'm here. Yep.

JAMES: Think you dropped out … First thing—

LACHLAN: No, I'm here.

JAMES: 'Kay, first thing, ah, Jodee has promised that there will be seventy-five million—

LACHLAN: I'm here.

JAMES: Yeah. We've got you, Lachlan. So Jodee has promised that there will be seventy-five million—

LACHLAN: Sorry. Yep.

JAMES: It's cool. A lag on the … Jodee has promised that there will be seventy-five million dollars in the bank at the end of June. Clearly he can't keep that promise now.

JODEE: The rights issue will keep us buoyant. Our major shareholders are doing exactly the right thing seeing us through. We are on track.

JAMES: We're out of cash. That's what this PBL cash review tells us.

LACHLAN: We're out of cash.

JAMES: We're going with the PBL cash / review.

LACHLAN: / The PBL cash review—yep.

JODEE: We have twenty million. I accept that is lower than expected.

JAMES: I'm not seeing that we even have that. Something's amiss because I'm seeing that we have twenty-one million owing to Optus and Telstra …

JODEE: There is a dispute with Telstra. I am contesting that.

LACHLAN: It's unacceptable for this to have happened.

JODEE: The real issue is timing; we're owed bills because the billing system failed. That will correct in the coming months. Our system has three months of billing caught up in it. That's cash. Everyone is so anxious about cash.

JAMES: Look, can we just stick to—

LACHLAN: We—yep—

JAMES: The first thing is—

LACHLAN: Go ahead, James.

JAMES: We agree on the cash injection that you and I discussed in France, Lachlan.

LACHLAN: Let's agree on the—ah-hah.

JAMES: I flew to Cannes to see Lachlan and Rupert. We confirmed we will raise one hundred-and-thirty-two million to refinance. PBL and News will fully underwrite the deal.

LACHLAN: A one-off.

JAMES: Just wanna repeat that, Lachlan?

LACHLAN: Ah, it's responsible. We're prepared to do this— [*Hearing* JAMES] Sure, yeah. Ah, it's responsible. We're prepared to do this but can we have it noted please that News Limited are surprised, we're disappointed, and upset to be asked to make this rescue?

JAMES: And PBL. The same. State the same for PBL. Surprised …

LACHLAN: Surprised …

JAMES: Disappointed …

LACHLAN: Disappointed …

JAMES: Yep. And upset.

LACHLAN: And upset.

JAMES and LACHLAN: [*together*] Yep.

JAMES: Now, this isn't easy. Jodee and I have spoken. Jodee has been a brother to me. That isn't for the minutes. This isn't easy. For the minutes, and I'm reading so we get this, I want now to thank Jodee Rich for his enormous entrepreneurial vision and hard work which has taken the company from its small beginnings to the global organisation that it is today. Today—

LACHLAN: Yeah—

JAMES: Today marks a new beginning for One.Tel—

LACHLAN: Sorry, James, just there, I'll express News Limited's gratitude for the passion and energy of Jodee Rich.

JAMES: Yep. Of course.

JODEE: Thank you. I appreciate that.

JAMES: So we're—

LACHLAN: News Limited accepts this resignation with mixed emotion.

JODEE: Ah, no, I haven't offered to resign.

JAMES: What? Yes you have.

LACHLAN: You have created remarkable value over the last six years.

JODEE: I believe I should stay.

JAMES: Jodee?

LACHLAN: What?

JODEE: I'm the only person with the knowledge—the confidence—

LACHLAN: Have I got this wrong? Aren't we already agreed on this?

JAMES: Yeah, I dunno what's happening here. Jodee told me he understood.

JODEE: You came to me crying, James—

JAMES: I wasn't crying.

JODEE: Yesterday. I told you I would do what's best for the company.

LACHLAN: Um, in that case— /

JAMES: No, Jodee— /

LACHLAN: —I take back everything I have said praising Jodee Rich. I take it back.

JODEE: I hope you are joking. Is he joking?

JAMES: Jodee, you knew this was coming.

LACHLAN: Yeah, no, let the minutes state that Lachlan Murdoch is not joking.

JODEE: Put on the record that I feel incredibly strongly that I shouldn't go. Yes the dinosaurs are getting restless but this is with you, you guys own this, so where do you want to be in twenty years? James, you know this, one of these days you're going to have to deny—

JAMES: Jodee. You're gone. Mate. Don't. Fuck. Just go.

JODEE: Right. I see. Alright, James, alright, mate. Now? Just go now?

JAMES: Yeah. Yes.

JODEE: I believed in you—even when you didn't.

JAMES: Get the door there for him, please.

JODEE: Call me, will you call me?

>Silence. JODEE *collects his laptop bag.*

LACHLAN: Jesus. You'd have Buckley's reaching him on a One.Tel phone anyway.

JODEE: Funny. Add to the indecency of this, Lachlan.

>Silence. JODEE *remembers to collect his rollerblades.*

LACHLAN: Oh, is he still there?

JODEE: Yes. Get this lawyer out of the way. Fuck off. Why don't you just fuck off?

JAMES: Alright, Jodee.

>JODEE *exits.*

LACHLAN: Like trying to kill—I dunno—something that just won't die.

JAMES: Can we—let's move on. We have to deal with the cash.

LACHLAN: Like a cockroach or a …

JAMES: We really need to—

LACHLAN: … a perianal wart.

JAMES: We really need to align ourselves—

LACHLAN: Guys, we need to better resource PR.

JAMES: We need a proper prospectus before a rights issue goes ahead.

LACHLAN: We need—

JAMES: It will need to be independent.

LACHLAN: A full prospectus, yeah.

JAMES: Full and independent.

LACHLAN: To see the full picture.

JAMES: I wasn't crying. I don't know what he—

LACHLAN: Not just flash reports. All of it.

JAMES: When are you back from New York, Lachlan?

LACHLAN: We should have resourced PR long ago. Hey? Oh, I'm coming back like now.

SCENE FIVE

JAMES *and* LACHLAN *meet in* LACHLAN*'s kitchen.*

JAMES: That's a big fridge you have there, Lachie. Is that Smeg?

LACHLAN: Yeah. Westinghouse.

JAMES: Okay.

LACHLAN: I think this fridge is new.

JAMES: Your wife buy it?

LACHLAN: Someone chose all that stuff. The interior designer. I read that your uncle Clyde …

JAMES: Yeah, mate.

LACHLAN: Peacefully, mate?

JAMES: I think relatively peacefully. Yeah, I mean I think it's, you know and I'm sure it's never perfect. His heart, mate.

LACHLAN: You'll have a service here—

JAMES: Yeah.

LACHLAN: Or the States?

> A MAN *appears in a crisp shirt and black tie from another era. He could be Clyde Packer's ghost. He is more likely to be a member of Lachlan's household staff. He is invisible to them. As*

they talk, he wipes a bench and leaves a bowl of nuts for them. He disappears.

JAMES: A memorial in Woollahra. Dad's going to be there. Kerry's pretty sick. Worse than the media knows, but I think …

LACHLAN: And this stress.

JAMES: He's bouncing back. Amazing how he can. I'll get Kerry to his brother's memorial. He loved Clyde. I find it very moving this show of, this togetherness now, family and—the thing is, at the end of the day, my family, there's so much love, that's the thing.

LACHLAN: Yeah.

JAMES: Yeah. I could pick up a fridge like that. I need a big fridge like that.

LACHLAN: We both need a beer.

JAMES: Yeah.

LACHLAN: Fuck the fridge. It's—

JAMES: Yep.

LACHLAN: [*swinging open the fridge door*] It's what's inside that—

JAMES *blubbers tears.*

Come on, Jamie. Come on now, mate.

JAMES *can't stop crying.*

JAMES: Worthless. I'm … just …

LACHLAN: You're not. You're stressed.

JAMES: I was wrong.

LACHLAN: About what?

JAMES: It's worthless. Worthless.

LACHLAN: What's …?

JAMES: This money that they said is caught up in the billing system—

LACHLAN: Fuck.

JAMES: It's—

LACHLAN: Fuck. What have they found?

JAMES: There's one hundred and sixty million, but it's not all collectable.

LACHLAN: There's a collections department.

JAMES: It's mostly bad debts.

LACHLAN: There are provisions for that.

JAMES: No. The provisions are too low. I mean this is what happens when you try to provide, y'know, to single mothers or apprentices, surfie wankers and junkies, these, you know, these caravan park bludgers, they were signing them all up. Fuckin'. Stupid incentives to sign up these losers because these fakes, these dealers who stole from us—they've found customer accounts named Fred Flintstone and bullshit. Fucking Astro Boy.

LACHLAN: Fuck. We'll have to lay off fucking staff. How many can we cull?

JAMES: I'd like to.

LACHLAN: We've invested close to—together it's up near a billion. Where were the controls? I thought there were controls.

JAMES: I'd like to take charge.

LACHLAN: God.

JAMES: I'm worried Dad will make me call it quits now.

LACHLAN: Call what quits?

JAMES: I could turn the business cash positive, Lachlan. It might only take three hundred million all up. That gives us six months. It's not much more than the rescue bid.

LACHLAN: More? I can't. One.Tel doesn't mean enough to Dad.

JAMES: Don't we mean enough?

LACHLAN: You'll never convince Kerry for more. We have to pull the rescue bid. Don't we?

JAMES: We're their sons, their boys.

LACHLAN: James, I have to be clear, right now, this is the first moment that Lachlan Murdoch has been made aware that One.Tel can't pay debts. Okay? I am noting that. I am not accusing you, James, but I have been misled.

JAMES: Not by me.

LACHLAN: I'll use my best endeavours to protect you.

JAMES: Say it. Not by me.

LACHLAN: I know how genuine you are. You championed this thing.

JAMES: We championed this thing.

LACHLAN: I relied on you, James.

JAMES: You were here too.

LACHLAN: Hey. Hey. We have to be smart now. People trusted us and they invested. Some people can't afford to lose money.

JAMES: I can't afford to lose money. Are we fucked?

LACHLAN: Let's get some of the boys around here to strategise. We have to get it out there that we were profoundly misled. Alright. Jamie? James? You alright?

JAMES: No.

LACHLAN: No. Okay.

JAMES: I can't face Dad.

LACHLAN: Yes you can.

JAMES: Dad knows what this does to me. My marriage is ending.

LACHLAN: Hey? Oh shit, man.

JAMES: I'm just not a very pleasant man to be around. She always hated it how … I don't know if your dad calls you after midnight to debate. Kerry screams at me. Most nights. I scream at her most mornings because of that.

LACHLAN: Marriage is— /

JAMES: And— / Yeah?

LACHLAN: What were you going to say?

JAMES: Just, she's my absolute soulmate.

LACHLAN: Yeah?

JAMES: Yeah. I thought for a moment it was what happiness must feel like. But despite everything I can give her, she'll still leave me and that can only mean I'm really not worth it.

> JAMES *takes a handful of nuts.*

LACHLAN: Nah, mate.

JAMES: Maybe if One.Tel had rebounded—or the advertising revenue at Nine—my marriage would have been rescued, but the stress kills things. Y'see, no-one in my family has ever been smashed about like this, Lachlan.

> CLYDE PACKER'S GHOST *returns in the guise of Lachlan's house-hold staff.*

LACHLAN: I bet they've all had—we all have our …

JAMES: But this is so undignified. You can't even rig up the exhaust fumes to the driver's seat of your Jaguar—not when you have a driver.

LACHLAN: What?

JAMES: No no, because suicide is undignified—was joking. Those smart cars would detect it. It's cowardly and selfish.

LACHLAN: Yeah, no, Jamie, you would never …

JAMES: I'm just hungry.

LACHLAN: Don't ever do that.

JAMES: Nah, I know. You got ice cream in here, Lachie?

LACHLAN: Have a look. Jamie, some of this is just … All things pass. Nothing stays.

JAMES: My family's fortune started when my great grandfather found a single penny at the Hobart racetrack and put it down twenty-to-one. Just a lucky break and …

CLYDE PACKER'S GHOST *places coasters. He locks eyes on* JAMES.

GHOST: Will there be anything else?

JAMES: What, what are you saying?

GHOST: Nothing more for you. Nothing.

JAMES: What's he mean by that? Fuck.

LACHLAN: Jamie, mate, just asking if you want any—want some water maybe?

JAMES: No I'm … Don't need …

LACHLAN: I think we're right, thanks.

CLYDE PACKER'S GHOST *leaves.*

Jamie, you're just …

JAMES: Like, maybe Burger Rings?

LACHLAN: I don't think we have them.

JAMES: It's alright then.

LACHLAN: It doesn't end with this. Right? Right?

JAMES: What will your dad do to you?

LACHLAN: He um … he doesn't raise his voice. He doesn't need to.

JAMES: I have this fantasy.

LACHLAN: We should make calls.

JAMES: I live out the remainder of life on this beautiful stunning yacht. It would be a Mangusta 165. I'd be speeding along with some mates off Portofino.

LACHLAN: You could.

JAMES: I wish.

LACHLAN: At any point just pick up the phone, withdraw. We're hurting, mate, but we're never going to be eating out of bins.

JAMES: This boat I am talking about is very expensive.

> JAMES *eats ice cream from the container. He does not offer any to* LACHLAN.

LACHLAN: Y'know the thing about our fathers? They know we are them. I'm him. The future him. So are my siblings so … For you it's simpler; it's just you—

JAMES: And Gretel. I have an older sister.

LACHLAN: Oh, sure. I know. But your dad isn't giving her a hard time. He knows you have to become him. And you will, James. You'll be him. He might bite your head off first, but he can't get in the way of what you want: to be him after he goes. Bigger than him.

JAMES: The yacht's fifty mil with the engine I'd want and all the extras. Over fifty. The fastest dinghy in the Med, if you can imagine.

LACHLAN: But really, there's something—sometimes only we know it because we've seen Dad frail and losing arguments with Mum. They're not gods. And they make big mistakes too. All the time.

JAMES: My father is a great man. He trebled his privileged start twice over. He perfected Nine, reformed world cricket and everything else. He is a brilliant strategist and nobody can diminish his commitment and service to this country. I will never achieve anything as great as what Kerry created.

LACHLAN: Then give up. You're torturing yourself. Go dive off that yacht somewhere.

> JAMES *is eating all the ice cream.*

SCENE SIX

YOUNG KERRY *spews, taking punches to the stomach.* CLYDE'S GHOST *watches.* FRANK *calls for* KERRY. *A helicopter churns. And the* LITTLE BOY *holds a broken tennis racket.*

Bondi. A darkened room. JAMES *is shrouded in a doona.*

There is a cigarette in an ashtray on the opposite side of the room. JAMES *cannot stand up. The cigarette smoke snakes.* JAMES *stands. A voice bellows for him.*

KERRY: [*offstage*] James! James! Where is he?!

> JAMES *winces. Dad's coming for him.*

Where is he in this damn—damn maze! James, you answer me, son!
James!

JAMES: Dad. In here. I am in here.

>   KERRY *enters in a suit. He takes off the hat he's wearing.*

KERRY: What's going on?

JAMES: Dad …

KERRY: It stinks in here.

>   KERRY *lets in some air, some light.*

Have you been avoiding me?

JAMES: Phone's … landline has to be reconnected and I'm switching
over the mobile.

>   JAMES *goes to kiss his father.*

KERRY: What are you doing? Can't kiss me. My cheeks bleed. You can't
be late to this. How pissed did you get?

JAMES: No. Not much. I …

KERRY: I can smell it on you.

>   *He wipes his cheek with his handkerchief.*

This is from all the medication. The steroid prednisone. It's a fucking
horror show. My face is like vellum.

>   *The handkerchief is reddened.*

[*His hat*] Even daylight's trying to end me.

JAMES: So long as you're not in pain.

KERRY: No no, I've had five years added to my life. I was right. Nobody
was listening to me, but I was right. My doctors think it is a fucking
miracle. I even took myself whoring again. Strip off and get into the
shower. You can't be late.

>   JAMES *checks his wrist—he no longer wears a watch. He searches
>   for something within his doona.*

JAMES: Where's my … my phone?

KERRY: You told me it doesn't work.

JAMES: To check the time.

>   KERRY *looks at his watch.*

KERRY: Noon.

JAMES: Already?

KERRY: I jotted a speech for you to read.

JAMES: I didn't know if I was … Thought you'd be speaking.

KERRY: You don't get out of it that easy, son. What stinks? Go clean your teeth.

JAMES: Rupert released a statement.

KERRY: Christ, is it me? Wait a minute while I find a Mintie.

> KERRY *fishes a Mintie out of his pocket.*

JAMES: Rupert is sharing the blame with Lachlan.

KERRY: So he fucking should. Where was Rupert? Where was Lachlan?

> KERRY *unwraps the lolly and pops it in his mouth.*

JAMES: The media are circling, Dad. There are ways to frame this at the shareholders' meeting. I'm not telling you what to say but it's important that they hear you still back me.

KERRY: I'm not going to the shareholders' briefing.

JAMES: Not going?

KERRY: You'll address them. You'll accept full blame. Get ready.

> *A bottle of vodka rolls from the doona.*

We'll get you coffee. You need to hurry.

JAMES: Dad, look, I accept I made mistakes. Big mistakes. But if they look at Crown—no-one's paying attention to the casino side because they prefer that, Dad, they prefer the story of me failing. Branding me. A loser. And I am not a loser. I ran every decision by you. You backed this. You championed this too and—

KERRY: Are you making an accusation?

JAMES: No. I'm … We both could have done more to understand how a telco works. That's all I am saying.

KERRY: Well, don't go saying it. It is fanciful to say that. You never had anything but a limp grip on management.

JAMES: I know, but—

KERRY: You know? You let the company overspend like a complete fuckwit.

JAMES: So why didn't you stop me?

KERRY: What? What did you say to me?

JAMES: You were so certain. Did you want me to fail?

KERRY: You are inconsistent. You are just plain inconsistent. You want your autonomy and you want everything to be my fault. You claimed the credit with lightning fucking alacrity when its share price was inflated. Now you think I should hold your fucking hand and I am not, no. You, you fucked up. You ran out of cash. You fall for people; you get besotted by salesmen. Why is that? Why? Haven't I taught you anything?

JAMES: I don't know.

KERRY: Yes you do. Control is what matters.

JAMES: And I'm not in control.

KERRY: I fucking know that much, son. People need to know who is in charge. You'll do your mea culpa today and then I'm stepping in again. I won't have you destroy my reputation, not at this late stage, son. I have worked too hard for this name.

JAMES: And my name?

KERRY: There'll be no more fuck-ups. The market needs peace of mind. I've already found buyers for eBay and the rest of this new media fairyland. [*The Mintie*] Fuck, I'm about to lose a fucking molar to this thing.

He works away at his teeth.

As for that ANZ loan, James, I looked into it. You'll pay that back yourself.

KERRY *wipes his hand somewhere.*

JAMES: I don't have the funds.

KERRY *spits into his handkerchief.*

KERRY: Ah, look at that. Disgusting.

JAMES: Dad, I can't pay it back, not now.

KERRY: Sell something. Your wedding ring for a start.

JAMES: Shit, Dad.

KERRY: What happened there, son? I would have liked a crack at her myself.

JAMES: It's killing me. Get me through this. You have to.

KERRY: Absolutely not. You are going to learn a lesson.

JAMES: But I can't. I can't. I can't sleep. I never sleep.

KERRY: And my face bleeds when I sweat. Man up.

JAMES: My brain won't shut off. You're always on my shoulders.

KERRY: Other way around I think you'll find, son.

JAMES: Listen. Listen to me. I'm breaking. I'm broken. Last night

I prayed. I kept praying and praying to God, but I didn't get an answer.

KERRY: Ha. I've been to the other side, son, and let me tell you there's fucking nothing there.

JAMES: So what's stopping me ending it all? Hey? That'd be easier. I could just end it.

Silence.

Because One.Tel was supposed to be about how we'd go on into the future. I had all these thoughts hitting me last night about what it was going to be and how I was steering it, for you. Even saw the house I'd be living in, with my kids. And I thought about that moment when Telstra came knocking and I thought, did Dad know … Maybe Dad always knew that was our departure point when the price was so high. We'd be out there now buying in the downturn. Did you? You knew that the sale would collapse at eighteen a share. Couldn't bear it. Couldn't bear it if I was the one to sell. You didn't want me to win.

KERRY: No, son.

JAMES: No?

KERRY: No. I thought you were going to win.

JAMES: I was trying to make our future and if there is no future now, if I am too much of a fuckwit then what am I doing here because there's only misery watching it all end with me? It's killing me and it is just going to keep on killing me if I can't win, can't get a win. Because, even with the casinos raking it in with—literally punters pouring their pockets into our profits—no-one sees me winning. No-one. Dad, last night, I polished off that fuckin' vodka there and I got really fucking close to …

Silence. JAMES *buckles.* KERRY *goes to him. He holds his son.*

I stink. I think I must have vomited somewhere here. I was close to just … just kissing it all goodbye.

KERRY: I think you should.

JAMES *looks his father in the eye.*

Where would you prefer to be? Take the boat. Go somewhere.

JAMES: I … I don't know …

KERRY: Somewhere that's … The polo fields in Argentina or on the boat. Go.

JAMES: But the shareholders' meeting today—I have to …

KERRY: Not if it's going to kill you, you don't.

JAMES: You'd let me just …?

KERRY: Take the *Arctic P*. Where's it docked now?

JAMES: Maldives, isn't it?

KERRY: Send for it. Get it back here.

JAMES: Or I could charter a … I could just fly there.

KERRY: That's right. You could. Do that.

JAMES: What, now? Just … just take off? The press would think, they'd think I'm not coming back.

KERRY: If the media are worrying you, cleave off the surname. James Bloggs. Nobody is interested in James Bloggs.

JAMES: Are you cutting me off? Is it—am I done? You're punishing me.

KERRY: I'm going to have to go and speak to the shareholders now.

JAMES: It isn't fair to just cut me off. Don't. Is that what you are doing? You are dumping me? Just firing me.

KERRY: Calm down, will you? Nobody is doing that. If you need to get away then that is what you should do. You are free to go. Nobody wants this to kill you, James. What would you like me to say on your behalf?

JAMES: Say?

KERRY: I'll have to make an excuse at the shareholders' briefing. Or do I just not mention you at all?

JAMES: Tell them … I wanted to face their questions but … I wanted to explain why the … that I accept errors were made and that …

KERRY: You have snot there. Wipe that snot away.

JAMES: Tell them, that, say, I am doing what I can to learn from those mistakes … but for the moment I … I don't know if it's a spiritual kind of … I want them to know that the casinos are strong and that the government is one hundred percent behind us on that and … Sydney has been good to our family so I … I don't want to be the one who … There's still the gaming and it's growing and if the Chinese middle class really … Sydney is my … We could build more … Say, just say to them that … I want you to say you believe in me. Someone has to believe in me. I might be a fuckwit but I am not a liar. My mistake was I was a believer. I'm …

*The cigarette is hanging from the edge of the ashtray with a trail
of smoke, well out of reach.*

I'm sorry I've done this to you.

JAMES *gets himself that cigarette.*

I know. I have to front up there today. Just me. To be my own man.
My own man. By myself. To own it. I owe you that. And I think I need
it because … I want it.

KERRY *puts on his hat to leave.* JAMES' *hands are shaking.*

I want that. I want it. I want. I want. I want.

His father, his grandfather, is his shadow. JAMES *smokes the entire
cigarette.*

THE END